To Shana Tate—

Happiness
        and
                Success always,

Donald Curtis
        3/8/96

Happiness and Success through
through
Personal Power

HAPPINESS & SUCCESS
through
PERSONAL POWER

Training & Ten Steps

DONALD CURTIS

 DeVorss & Company, Publishers

Formerly *How to Be Happy and Successful*
and *Ten Steps to Personal Power*

ISBN: 0-87516-629-6
Library of Congress Card Catalog No. 90-84239

Printed in the United States of America

DEVORSS & COMPANY
BOX 550, MARINA DEL REY, CA 90294-0550

Contents

Part II: Ten Steps

Happiness & Success through
Personal Power

Part I: Training

What Is Happy,
Successful Living?

ABRAHAM LINCOLN said, "Most people are just about as happy as they make up their minds to be." The same observation is true about success. Happiness and success do not just happen. They are the effect of what we are inside; they are projections of states of consciousness.

Therefore, by unfolding spiritually, by developing mentally, and by maturing emotionally, we develop those inner causes which produce outer results — in terms of happiness and success. Inner harmony and balance produce outer peace and order — aspects of happiness and success.

Jesus said, "Seek ye first the kingdom of God and His righteousness, and all of these things shall be added unto you." He also said, "The kingdom of God is within you," and "It is the Father's good pleasure to give you the Kingdom." Therefore, it would seem that what we are seeking for we already have, and if we recognize this, that which we greatly desire — happiness and success — come about naturally. Sounds reasonable, doesn't it? Let's try it.

Let us endeavor to fulfill those personal requirements which ensure the rich, full life. No one else can make us happy and successful. This is a do-it-yourself proposition. Each one of us has dominion:

> I am the master of my fate;
> I am the captain of my soul.
> — William Ernest Henley, *Invictus*

But let us remember: "The kingdom of heaven is not taken by storm." "Neither lo here, nor lo there, but behold, the Kingdom of God is within you," and "Not by might, nor by power, but by my spirit, saith the Lord of hosts."

Our happiness and our success are woven out of the fabric of our daily attitudes, thoughts, feelings, opinions, actions and reactions. All of these we can do something about. We can control them, develop them and channel them. There is no secret to happy, successful living. It is simply this: BECOME HAPPY AND SUCCESSFUL INSIDE AND YOU WILL BE HAPPY AND SUCCESSFUL OUTSIDE.

It is with this "becoming" that we are concerned in this little guidebook to happiness and success. The suggestions in these brief chapters are simple, but the results from practicing them can be tremendous. It is up to you. You must follow the Steps,*

---

*See Part II: "Ten Steps."

but, believe me, you will find that the effort and discipline which you put forth will pay tremendous dividends.

Just remember, if we are to be happy and successful, it is not so much outer doing as inner being. The instruction of the Master is unmistakable. "Be ye therefore perfect, even as your Father in heaven is perfect."

Underlying the techniques given here is emphasis upon the Inner Presence — the Kingdom of God within. As we touch this Center, and recognize our Oneness with God, we grow in our consciousness of wholeness. This consciousness is the source of successful, happy living.

1

If You Would Be Happy . . .

THESE BASIC steps toward happiness are simple, even though sometimes difficult to carry through.

Number One: LEARN TO GET ALONG
               WITH YOURSELF

Number Two: LEARN TO GET ALONG
               WITH OTHER PEOPLE

Number Three: GO INTO PARTNERSHIP
               WITH GOD

Number Four: LOOK FOR THE GOOD
               IN EVERY PERSON AND
               IN EVERY SITUATION

Number Five: DO SOME GOOD FOR SOME-
               ONE EVERY DAY

Number Six: USE THE POWER OF PRAISE

Get Along with Yourself

If you can get along with yourself, you have taken a great step toward happiness. Our struggles, our animosities, our frustrations really arise from within. We are disappointed with ourselves sometimes, and proceed to take out our disappointment on other people. If we have not been able to achieve what we want in life—if we become embittered because things have not gone just the way we want them to go— we have a way of becoming critical and hostile toward other people. *If we are to find the road to happiness, we need to accept ourselves, not egotistically, but with a deep understanding and appreciation of what we really are.*

First of all, we are created in the image and likeness of God. Do you know what that really means? We are one with the great Creative Power of the Universe. This Power flows through us and through our affairs. It is the gift of God to every man. It is responsive to us as individuals, for EACH OF US IS AN INDIVIDUALIZED EXPRESSION OF THE UNIVERSAL.

Every single one of us is a unique and wonderful human being. Take yourself, for example. There is no other person in the world like you. There never has been. There never will be. You have a special contribution to make to life—one that no other person can make.

It is important that each of us accept himself as the kind of individual described above, with freedom of choice to fulfill his highest destiny or to be submerged in a sea of negativity. The choice is ours. If we choose the former, we will feel ourselves surrounded by the love and the wisdom of God. We will forgive ourselves as well as others when we have made seeming mistakes. (You have no idea how important this is.) We will know also that the great Creative Power within is working for our good in every possible way.

There is much to learn about how to work with this Power. For the present, however, it is enough to know that the Creative Power of the Universe, acting as love and as law, is constantly flowing through us and through our affairs. This Power is released most abundantly when, simply and humbly, we accept ourselves as people of worth and dignity, surrounded and indwelt by the peace and the power, the love and the wisdom of the Indwelling Christ.

Get Along with Others

The second basic step toward happiness is to learn to GET ALONG WITH OTHER PEOPLE. A recent survey in industry showed that the biggest cause of job turnover is the inability to get along with other people. We get along with other people by understanding and appreciating them. Our friend the American Indian says, "Never judge a man until you have walked a mile in his moccasins." It helps to think of other people as being like ourselves. They have problems, goals, ambitions, appetites, desires, weaknesses, strengths just as we have—many of these the same as ours.

More and more we come to realize that man is a wonderful being. Shakespeare says:

What a piece of work is man! how noble in reason! how infinite in faculty! in form and moving how express and admirable! in action how like an angel! in apprehension how like a god!

When we learn to feel this way about other people—even though we may not *like them*—we not only get along with them, but we have happiness within ourselves. It is a marvelous challenge—isn't it?—to accept other people as we accept ourselves. We salute the Christ in others as we become increasingly aware of this Presence within ourselves. In this way, we learn to get along with ourselves and with others, and the natural result is greater happiness and success in everyday living.

Go into Partnership with God

The third basic step toward attaining happiness is to GO INTO PARTNERSHIP WITH GOD. God is the Senior Partner in every life, in every marriage, in every firm, in every endeavor—the Divine Spark in each of us.

This Senior Partner wants us to have all the breaks—wants us to get all the credit. God wants us to be happy and successful. This loving Father is our friend and guide, the Infinite Healing Presence within each one of us. Talk things over with the Boss every morning and several times during the day.

But a partnership is a two-way street. We as individuals have certain responsibilities, too. What kinds of thoughts and feelings are predominant in our lives? Do we think about happy, harmonious situations until we can actually feel such experiences? If one door is closed to us, do we turn with faith to something else? If we awaken in the night, do we turn and toss with worry? Or do we quietly turn our thoughts to happy, peaceful situations in the past, or imagine clearly and vividly happy situations we would like to experience in the future? When we accept our responsibilities, the feeling of partnership with God is a tremendous step toward happiness.

Look for the Good in Every Situation

Sometimes we have to deal with seemingly negative situations, but it is possible to deal with them positively. This brings us to our fourth step: LOOK FOR THE GOOD IN EVERY PERSON AND IN EVERY SITUATION. This does not mean that we put our reason and our judgment in our pockets. We simply look through outer appearances until we can see God there, not only as Law but as the Infinite Healing Presence.

We have a way of experiencing just about what

we expect. If we see the negative and the unhappy, the tense and the troubled areas of life, those are the kinds of experiences that come back to us. But this law of happiness says, "LOOK FOR THE GOOD. LOOK FOR THE BEST YOU CAN FIND."

There isn't a situation anywhere that doesn't have some good in it. There isn't a person anywhere that doesn't have good in him. Learn to look for the good, and good will return to you. *No matter what the problem may seem to be, God is already there.* There is a lesson for us in every situation. We are never confronted by a situation that we do not need as part of life itself. We grow through these experiences, and we are grateful for the good that comes from them.

Do a Good Deed Every Day

Number five is important, too: DO SOME GOOD FOR SOMEONE EVERY DAY. Let's all be Boy Scouts today, shall we? Have you done your good turn today? Well, start right now! Look for chances to be happy, to be courteous, to be kind. *Remember especially to be kind.* Do something for someone every day, without thought of return. Maybe you will send a wire to a friend congratulating him. Perhaps you will drop a note to someone who is not expecting to hear from you; but you do good by letting him know that you are thinking of him; that you recognize what he has done. And who gets the benefit of a good deed? Everyone! The one who does it most of all, when he gives without thought of return.

Use the Power of Praise

THE POWER OF PRAISE—what a gift this is! Truly, it is one of the greatest gifts we have. Look out upon the world and praise it. If you have a car that you are driving to work, praise this car before you get into it. Tell it it is going to take you to work safely. Tell it it is a good car. It doesn't matter if it is an old tin Lizzy—tell it it is a good one. Make it proud of itself.

Praise your secretary at the office. Praise your wife, or praise your husband right now. Praise the kids. *Look for something good and dwell on it.* When this is done, good has a way of expanding and flourishing. The power of praise is one of the highest powers that we have, but we often overlook it. It is free to everybody. Just praise! Tell even inanimate things how wonderful they are, and the Spirit within will respond. Praise is a powerful means of unlocking the door to happy living.

Meditation

And now let us be still and know these things, each one about himself. Today we are immersed in happiness; we live happily, and we live well, getting along with other people, learning to understand ourselves. We are in partnership with the Infinite Creative Presence, the mind of God within each person. We see the best in every situation. We spread good wherever we go, using the power of praise to bless our day. We give thanks that this is so. And so it is.

2

How to Accomplish Your Purpose

STUDY THESE four steps carefully. Tuck them into the back of your mind. Let them sink down into your subconscious. If you follow these steps, they will help you do what you want to do, be what you want to be, and accomplish the purposes that you set for yourself.

Number One: TAKE INVENTORY OF
                 YOURSELF

Number Two: DECIDE CLEARLY UPON
                 YOUR OBJECTIVE

Number Three: HAVE FAITH IN YOURSELF

Number Four: DO WHAT YOU HAVE TO DO

These steps are simple enough, aren't they?—clear, specific, and to the point. Let's look at them one by one.

Take Inventory of Yourself

As you take inventory of yourself, catalogue your abilities. Be truthful. It is not everyone who can be a great artist or a great speaker or writer. It is not everyone who can run a grocery store. It isn't everyone who can drive a truck. What is it that you can do? Be reasonable. What is your inclination? What are your tastes? What are your abilities? What were you put in this world to do?

It is important in taking inventory of ourselves to be completely honest. Every one of us isn't a world beater, you know. Our talents and our capacities may be fairly mediocre. If so, let's acknowledge it. On the other hand, let's not underrate ourselves. Each of us has some talent—something that he does especially well. *Whatever your ability may be— great or small—know that there is a need for it somewhere.*

In some cases it may be important to ask: "Have I stifled my real abilities? Have I kept my light under a bushel?" Maybe you have abilities which you have never used. Many people have, you know.

A person may have had an inclination in his early days to be an artist, or a writer, or a musican. But perhaps this person had to earn the living for the family: take care of a widowed mother or younger brothers and sisters. This person then put his real talent in the background and let the need of the moment govern him. Now sometime in his life this person needs to be honest with himself and say, "Am

I doing what I am supposed to do? How can I do the greatest good in my world? How can I best express myself?"

In this inventory, too, let us ask these questions: "Do I have certain character traits that it would be better to change? Am I too critical of others? Do I gossip or talk too much? Am I willing to take direction and suggestions from others?" Being willing to improve oneself is part of this first step in clearing the decks for achievement.

You can see that life is not just a matter of wandering about from pillar to post trying to find one's place in the world. *We find our right place when we decide what our purpose is.* To find this purpose we have to get acquainted with ourselves. This first step says, then: "Take inventory. Meet yourself face to face. Be honest! If there is something that needs to be changed, change it."

Only then are we ready for the next step.

Decide on Your Objective

Decide on your objective. How important this is! In the light of your abilities and interests, what do you want to accomplish? What do you want to have? What do you need? Be clear in your objective. Do you want to be a good artist, a good musician, a good writer, a good businessman, a good salesman, a good truck driver, a good housewife, a good mother, a good father — *a better person?*

From time to time each and every one of us has inclinations and desires in some of these directions, but we have to be specific. You can see what would happen if you went into a grocery store and carried on this kind of conversation with the clerk:

"I would like some groceries," you say.

"Well, what kind of groceries do you want: oatmeal, carrots, milk, yogurt, dried prunes? What is it that you want?" the clerk asks.

"Oh, just give me some stuff," you reply. "I need enough to feed a family of three or four people."

"Yes, lady, I'm glad to know about your personal affairs; but what exactly do you want today?"

At this point you would have to decide in what quantity you want some particular items or else go home hungry. You would be forced to be specific.

It is important to be specific in your objective. Faint heart never won fair lady, and a clouded mind never plotted a clear course through life. Decide what it is that you want to do. Do not be afraid to picture clearly, to form in your consciousness the image of the type of person you want to be. Of course, certain details of how this is to come about are left to the working of the Creative Law, but you must get things started. Our job is to decide WHAT! God's job is HOW to do it. Our responsibility is to have clearly in mind what it is that we want to do, what it is we want to have. Then we go ahead and put the creative machinery into operation. In our final two points we'll see how this is done.

Have Faith in Yourself

It is easy to say, "Have faith in yourself. Dissolve your doubts and transform them into courage and confidence." The question is: "How do we do this?" One of the best ways is to *strengthen your feeling that God is working through you.* You know how a plant always turns to the light to get the sunshine. Just so, *the Life Principle is forever turning us in the direction of our good.* God wants us to have what we need and what we want. The Infinite enjoys working through us. *The Universal is forever expressing through the individual.*

When we accept this partnership with God, we build up a personal conviction of confidence and assurance. It is important to dissolve the doubts, the little nibbling foxes that destroy our creative power and energy. Dissolve these and transform them into a conviction that God is working through you. *God is Life, Nature, Principle, Energy, Law.* All of these are working through you as an immutable force, as an all-powerful good.

As the doubts are dredged up and dissolved, the channel is opened through which this great Creative Force may work. Know this today! Know that God is working in your life right now. God is the Infinite Intelligence, the Great Healing Power, the great Builder, the Great Creator, the great DOER. He is a personal Presence in each individual, working as love and as law. He is not a person, but a Presence, an awareness. We build our relationship to this

Presence within our own hearts through prayer, through right thinking, through right living in our daily life.

Do What Needs to Be Done

Now go ahead and do what needs to be done. James in the Bible says, "Faith without works is dead." There comes a time when we must get out and get started. We must do the thing that we have planned to do. Make that telephone call today. Write that letter. Make an appointment for that interview. Go out and buy that gift. Put down on paper the plan for the company that you want to form. Do not put it off any longer. We have all the spiritual and mental strength we need. Let's go ahead and do what we have to do!

These four steps, when followed, are your keys to greater accomplishment:

TAKE INVENTORY OF YOURSELF

DECIDE CLEARLY UPON YOUR
    OBJECTIVE

HAVE FAITH IN YOURSELF

DO WHAT NEEDS TO BE DONE

Start today to follow through on these activities. They will lead the way to the accomplishment of your purpose.

Meditation

Let us be still for a moment. Taking inventory of ourselves, we find that we have abilities and talents that the world needs. We have great potential for good in whatever we do. We decide now to become aware of the possibilities which are ours. Today, as we go forward into our occupations, into our relations with people we meet, we are free from doubt. We are established in love and in faith. We do what we need to do with the conviction that God is working through us now. And so it is.

3

How to Get Along with People

How to get along with people is of interest to all of us. Here are five suggestions that will pay dividends:

Number One: BE APPRECIATIVE

Number Two: LISTEN TO PEOPLE

Number Three: FOLLOW THE GOLDEN RULE

Number Four: MIND YOUR OWN BUSINESS

Number Five: BE FRIENDLY

Be Appreciative

In getting along with people, nothing quite does what a good "thank you" will do. Perhaps it's a telephone call or a letter. Maybe it is just saying in person: "I appreciate what you have done. I certainly thank you for your interest. And that gift you gave me! It's lovely. And what a good time I had at your house. I wish we could be together more often."

Show appreciation. It doesn't have to be a letter. It doesn't have to be a return gift. Just show people that you like what they did. This old world of ours would spin on its axis much more smoothly if all of us could learn to show appreciation in friendly ways. Let's determine to do it today, shall we?

If a person is truly appreciative of life and what it offers, he will keep his complaints to a minimum. No one likes a complainer, a whiner, a person who gets hold of something that seems to be wrong and hangs on to it like a dog with a bone. If there is something that needs correction, see if you can do something about it. Go to the place or the person where help is needed. Do what you can to bring about good. Then release the situation to the Creative Law.

It is a good thing to count our blessings and keep complaints to a minimum. This attitude has a great deal to do with getting along with people. But being appreciative means even more. If we appreciate the wonder of human beings, we are *tolerant*. This word makes us think sometimes that we're looking down on other people—that we are "tolerating" people who are different from us in racial, religious, or ethnic backgrounds. But this is not what the word *tolerance* really means. *It means to see the other person's point of view and then to be considerate of it*. Give him a chance to make his point. It may bring you fresh insight. If we are tolerant in all ways, people will be tolerant of us. You see, we may have a lot of "sticky" points too, things that are not always easy to understand or put up with. We would like to have everyone give US the benefit of the doubt. Let's do the same thing! This all helps us to get along better with people.

Listen to People

The second point we want to make is simple but difficult. LISTEN to what people say and try to understand them. It has been estimated that we understand only about 30 percent or hear about 30 percent of what is said to us. Seventy percent, then, is not heard at all or is misunderstood. Do you listen to what your husband or your wife says when you are reading the paper, eating oatmeal or eggs, drinking coffee, thinking about getting in the car and out on the freeway?

You know this business of communication is most important in life — the endeavor to share our ideas with other people so that we can really understand what they are saying and they can understand what we say. All through the day when a person speaks to you, try to stop your own mental processes for a moment and give your undivided attention to that person.

Perhaps you have had occasion, as I have, to meet some of the great and the near-great in this world of ours. There is one thing which characterizes every one of them. Each gives his undivided attention to the particular task or incident at hand. If a person is talking to him, he listens with all of the understanding that he has. He makes an honest effort to assimilate what he hears. This is one of the greatest secrets in getting along with other people: *Give your undivided attention to them. Listen to them and really try to understand what they have to say.* This is a big step that will pay dividends in harmony and love throughout life.

Live by the Golden Rule

Another important step is to make an honest effort to LIVE BY THE GOLDEN RULE, "Do unto others as you would have others do unto you." We can interpret this very simply: If you are not willing to be hit in the face, do not hit another fellow in the face. If you are not willing to be stolen from, do not steal from another person. If you are not willing to be lied to, do not lie to another person.

Try sincerely to live by the Golden Rule. If you like kindness, consideration, politeness and love, show these qualities to other people. If you like to be listened to, if you like to be looked at with some degree of pleasantness and love, then do the same to other people. You see, we cannot have bitterness and resentment, unhappiness and negative criticism in our hearts and expect to get along with other people. They react to these feelings. But when we hold near and dear within our hearts those ideas and those principles which we would like to experience, other people respond accordingly. We find that we not only get along better with other people, we get along better with ourselves. This is the key: *Learn to get along with yourself and you will get along with other people,* because getting along with oneself helps one to be at peace with others.

Mind Your Own Business

I am not really saying this to YOU. I am saying it to ALL of us. Minding one's own business is a great help in getting along with people. We need to learn and to obey this bit of common sense. There is plenty for us to do. It is important to attend to our own affairs and make our own plans.

If a person asks for advice or calls us in for consultation, we will then have the energy and the interest to help him. But if we are always running about, minding everybody's business but our own, we are going to lose the race. We'll get stuck away back behind the finish line. Not only that, but we'll make some enemies along the way. Unasked-for advice can be very irritating. In getting along with people, it is good to mind one's own business. Now let's turn to our next suggestion.

Be Friendly

If we are friendly we are usually cheerful and congenial. It goes without saying that if we are truly cheerful and appreciative, we are going to fit into our surroundings. Most people will like us. They are going to invite us to social events. They are going to want us to work FOR them and WITH them. They are going to want to be around us.

A cheerful person develops an atmosphere about him that attracts friends. He "belongs" and fits into his world unless he is too "Pollyannaish" — too saccharinely sweet. This attitude drives people away; but if we are genuinely cheerful, we will have friends. Then, too, if we would have a friend, we should be one. And what is a friend? Someone has said that a *friend is somebody that knows all about us and likes us anyway.* This is our cue. Let's not just say, "I want friends" or "I need friends." Let's see if we can *be* a friend today — a friend to all humanity. But let's start right where we are. Think about your own household: husband or wife or children — mother, father, sister, or brother. Be a friend to them. Say, "What can I do for them? I love them. What can I do that they would appreciate?" Develop this idea of friendship today right where you are.

Meditation

Let us be still now for just a moment and turn to that quiet place within. We become increasingly aware of the Divine Spark within ourselves. We salute the Christ in every person we meet. We learn to love people—to understand them. We learn to build within ourselves this fiber of deep empathy and identification with our fellowman. We are one with each other, surrounded and indwelt by Infinite Love. We express love and understanding throughout this day and always. We give thanks that this is so. And so it is.

4

How to Be Healthy

W<small>E ALL</small> know that good health is a boon to happy, successful living. Here are five steps which lead to general good health:

Number One: BUILD A CONSCIOUSNESS OF HEALTH

Number Two: THINK AND SPEAK CON-STRUCTIVELY

Number Three: USE YOUR EMOTIONS CONSTRUCTIVELY

Number Four: TAKE CARE OF YOUR BODY

Number Five: LEARN TO PRAY AND LIVE AS A WHOLE BEING

Build a Consciousness of Health

To build a consciousness of health, there are certain things we should do and certain things we must not do.

First of all, think about the wonderful provisions that nature has made to nourish these bodies of ours and to keep them well. Not one of us could consciously digest his food, regulate his temperature, or keep the water content of the body constant. Some Power greater than we are does these things for us.

Our breathing, our circulation, our reflexes — over these, our conscious mind has no control. When sickness threatens, the forces of our bodies are mobilized to withstand the attack. There is a Power within our bodies that makes for inner balance (or homeostasis, if you prefer a technical word). This balance promotes health.

As you build a consciousness of health, *think of your body as the vehicle through which life expresses itself.* Praise your body for the service that it gives you. Become more aware all the time of the Infinite Healing Presence which flows through every cell of your body, invigorating and blessing you with Its healing currents.

See yourself in your imagination carrying on your daily activities in the full vigor of life until your cycle of experience on this plane is completed. Do not dwell in conversation or thought upon ailments, pills, doctors, operations. Do not give verbal "organ" recitals! Do not dwell on how sick Mrs. X is, or how little can be done to cure certain diseases.

Open your mind to the influx of ideas that are vital, strong and life-giving. Let your mind be nourished by such ideas. Think, feel, and act HEALTH, knowing that God is the source from which it comes.

Because we have freedom of choice, we can provide channels through which the Infinite Healing Presence can flow; but in the final analysis it is God's power that heals, renews, invigorates and sustains our bodies. What responsibilities, then, does freedom of choice give us?

Think and Speak Constructively

We hear a great deal about positive thinking. Let's try it. Let us affirm good in our world and endeavor to look for the best in every person and in every situation. All these efforts help us to experience health. Our doctor friends, for instance, have come a long way in this direction with the development of psychosomatic medicine, which recognizes the interaction of mind and body.

Our thoughts should be constructive, affirmative, positive in nature, and they should build those things in life that we would like to have there. Do you know that *thought is the most powerful thing in the world?* Using our thought negatively, always looking at those things which are unlovely and negative, tears us down, because such thoughts create a drag. They are against the natural order of things.

If we believe with Thomas Troward that the aspects of Spirit are Life, Love, Light, Power, Peace, Beauty and Joy, this belief automatically creates attitudes that are health-giving.

To be healthy is to be whole. Certainly a person cannot experience health in his body if he is dealing with troubled, worrisome, anxious thoughts in his mind. The attitudes that we carry with us are built up as a result of the things which we normally entertain in our thought. Paul in the Bible said:

Whatsoever things are true, whatsoever things are honest, whatsoever things are just, whatsoever things are pure, whatsoever things are lovely, whatsoever things are of good report; if there be any virtue, and if there be any praise, think on these things.

Will you try it today? Will you just accept the fact that there is a relation between what you think and the way you feel? You will find that this is true.

Not only thoughts but words have power. No wonder we are warned to think before we speak. How many times have we talked about aches and pains and operations without ever thinking about the impression such words could make on our subconscious mind?

But the word can be used magnificently for health. The Bible says, "In the beginning was the

Word, and the Word was with God, and the Word was God." Everything that was accomplished was done by this Word which is God. This Word represents idea taking form. Use the Word, then, to express clearly and definitely the health which you want to experience in your life.

Do your treatment work aloud. VOICE praise and blessing in your prayer. *Make your healing treatment session a period of talking to God.* The Master told his disciples to go into the closet and close the door when they prayed, and said that the "Father which seeth in secret shall reward theee openly." I find that speaking our prayers and treatments aloud gives form and shape to our ideas. It helps us to sustain the thought. Remember these things when you treat yourself and others for health.

Use the Energy of Emotions Constructively

Now let us talk about *feeling* in our third step toward health. One of our jobs in becoming a healthy person is to develop inner feelings of peace, love and faith. You say, "Aha! Very good, but how do I go about it when so much tension and pressure and conflict are all around me? How do I develop an inner feeling of peace?"

Sit down several times each day and take time to be quiet. Develop an inner consciousness of peace. Say, *"Peace is in me now. Let the winds blow, and let the waves toss; I am at peace."* How do we get that way? By learning to get along with ourselves, with our world, and with other people. For this, we need to develop an inner feeling of love.

Now many people are a little thorny inside. They are irritable, and they mistrust other people. They would like to get even with the world for inadequacies of their own; and so the out-going emotion is not one of love. It cannot be, unless the indwelling feeling is one of love. Develop this feeling if you would be healthy.

Many times the cause of sickness can be traced to a negative emotional climate. As long as we are human, we are subject to human frailties: such feelings as fear, hostility, anger, discouragement, guilt. There is one simple way to use the energy of such emotions: *Affirm that the Power within is transforming these feelings into love and service for others.* Emotions cannot be changed by will power. But the energy of both positive and negative emotions can be used constructively.

"Love," as Paul said, *"is the fulfilling of the law."* I do not see how a person can be consistently healthy unless he has a feeling of love inside him.

But you may ask, "What are some techniques for building or releasing love?" One way is to build your faith. Learn to relate yourself to the great universe in which you live. *Know that God is your partner in every situation. Recognize that every person is an expression of God.* Levels of development may vary, but we should learn to look through outer appearances for the spark of Divinity in every person. As we have faith in God, faith in life, faith in ourselves and others, somehow love and peace are established within us. When our emotions are balanced and harmonized, the natural functions within the body are better regulated.

Take Care of Your Body

TAKE CARE OF YOUR BODY, OBEY THE LAWS OF DIET, EXERCISE AND REST. This would also include breathing and cleanliness, would it not? Obey the laws of diet! Do you understand about food? Do you know about the different elements? Do you know what carbohydrates are, what proteins are, what their balance should be in your diet? Do you know what good food supplements to use?

Some people say, "Well, just pray, just give a treatment. I'll eat hot dogs and I'll eat pickles, and I'll eat all the ice cream and all the meat and potatoes and cake and desserts, and drink anything I want. I don't have to worry about it. Just say a prayer for me."

This is nonsense. Why should you pray, identifying yourself with the higher power of perfection and good if you do not obey a few simple rules of common sense in the care of your own body? Learn how to eat! More people kill themselves with their teeth than in any other way. Can you expect a body to be healthy unless it is properly exercised and used, unless the different muscles and the different functions of the body are blended together into a harmonious whole?

Learn some simple setting-up exercises, some good stretching exercises. Learn to walk. Learn to breathe. Learn to fill yourself with the spirit of life! Learn when to rest, when to let go, when to be still, when to let God take over.

Learn to Pray and Live as a Whole Being

Learn to pray and live as a whole being, made up of spirit, mind and body. And what does this mean? Most of us think of ourselves as people of a certain height and weight, working in a certain job. We never really put ourselves together. Humpty Dumpty cannot be healthy, he cannot be happy and successful, he cannot be whole, unless he thinks of himself as a whole being: spirit, mind and body. You see, at the level of the Higher Self, in the upper reaches of consciousness, we are one with Spirit; we are one with God.

The Bible tells us that we are made in the image and likeness of God. *We are individual expressions of the great Intelligence which is God.* This is the Spirit within us. *Spirit is the Power which knows Itself.* Spirit is expressed through the conscious mind, which has the power of choice and initiative, the power to think, to reason, to comprehend. *A person cannot be healthy unless he sees that he is first of all a spiritual being as well as a mental and a physical being.*

Another aspect of the great Intelligence is our unconscious mind which is part of the great Creative Principle of the universe, which is forever at work creating circumstances according to personal and universal laws on many levels. *To the degree that we unite spirit and mind, we increase our sense of wholeness.*

We are not only spirit and mind, but also body. We are physical beings just as we are mental and spiritual beings. The body is the vehicle of Spirit, the means of expression on this plane. The Infinite Healing Presence flows through every cell of our bodies, keeping different organs and functions in balance, infusing them with life and vigor.

We see ourselves, then, as whole beings, made up of spirit, mind and body. As each of us learns to pray and to live as a whole being, he is strengthened and energized. Good health is the result.

Meditation

Let us be still as we feel the Infinite Healing Presence flowing through us. We think, feel, and speak constructively, expressing deep inner feelings of peace, love and faith. We are whole beings—spirit, mind and body. We are grateful for the wonder of our bodies, the power of thought, the energy of emotions. We use these wisely. We are grateful for the Universal Healing Power. As we obey the laws of common sense throughout this day, harmony, order, and right action are taking place through all that we do. And so it is.

5

Building a Happy Marriage

EACH PARTNER in the marriage must accept responsibility for the success of the partnership. Here are some pointers that will help.

Number One: HAVE GOOD MANNERS

Number Two: TALK THINGS OVER

Number Three: MAINTAIN ORDER, DISCI-
PLINE AND BEAUTY IN
THE HOME

Number Four: EXPRESS LOVE, MUTUAL
REGARD AND RESPECT

Number Five: PRAY TOGETHER

Whether married or not, let us think about these five points as guides which will open the way to richer, fuller living.

Have Good Manners

How important it is to have good manners in the home—to remember to be kind, to be thoughtful, to be considerate. How much it means for the man of the house to remember to speak softly—to be as kind to his children and to his wife as he is in a business conference with people who might be able to do him some financial good. Sometimes we put on our best manners when we are out in public and take them off when we come home. Many times strangers see a better part of ourselves than our intimates do.

Let us try today to have really good manners in our homes. Could we say "please" and "thank you" a little more often? Could we say, "What do you think about it?" or "That's an interesting point of view." Let's really listen to each member of our family even though the person is close to us and we think we are very familiar with his point of view. We may be surprised sometimes at the fresh viewpoint we get.

There are many simple little courtesies that make for good family living. It is a simple little thing for the husband to pull the chair out from the table and seat his wife; a simple little thing to listen to the young people around the table as they express their ideas. How much better it is for the husband to open the car door and see that his wife is safely inside, instead of honking the horn and yelling, "Get a move on, will you? How long are you going to be?" By the same token, it is a wise wife who is as careful not to keep her husband waiting unnecessarily as she would be if a good friend were waiting. All of these little things are important, because *good manners help to make good marriages, and good marriages make life very good indeed.*

Talk Things Over

It has been said by those who have studied marital problems that part of the trouble with marriages that go wrong is that the partners have not established a proper basis for communication. They don't talk things over with each other. When they do not do this, how are they to know what each thinks, what each feels?

Let us start a plan right now. Suppose you and your husband or wife sit down at the breakfast table together every morning and talk things over. Plan the day. Get interested in each other all over again. Ask some questions that will show that you respect the other's point of view. Discuss those cherished plans. Are you going to buy a new car? Are you looking for a new home? Are you going to buy Junior a new suit? What about sister's graduation? What about the wedding that you are to attend? How about going to church together this Sunday? Talk over all of these things because they are important. They are part of the living, vital relationship which goes to make up a marriage.

Then we find little faults in each other occasionally, don't we? We disagree with the way the other person thinks or the way he speaks or what he does. These difficulties can often be overcome if we simply sit down and talk them over. Bring them into the open, not to nag about, but to resolve. When we express our feelings honestly and sincerely, then we are free inside and the misunderstanding doesn't rankle. It doesn't fester there to cause trouble later.

If there are real arguments or quarrels — and these things do arise — we need to learn how to handle them constructively. *Our difficulties diminish if we learn to talk them over objectively.* Concentrate on the solution to the problem, not on personalities. If you have felt resentment in the past, transform it into forgiveness and love. In your imagination relive the situation in love. If resentment occurs now, sit right down and talk it over. The end of the day is a good time to do this. Perhaps you will choose the quiet period in the evening or the time just before retiring. Then your talk together logically blends into a quiet time of reflection — many times into actual prayer.

To have this mutual trust, to talk over a difficulty, to see what your partner thinks about it — this is a wonderful husband-wife relationship. Try it!

Maintain Order and Beauty in the Home

It is said that order is heaven's first law. It is good to have order in the home: everything in its right place, a certain schedule as to when things are to be done. When are you to have breakfast? When are you to have dinner? When is Junior to do certain things? These arrangements should not be inflexible, but they should set up order so that people know what to expect. Discipline is important. Children respect discipline. They need it and they love it.

Then a sense of beauty in the home is important: good music, good books, good pictures, good furnishings. But most important of all is the beauty that comes from the human soul—the love and beauty that ray out from within as we share the good things of life with each other.

Express Love and Respect for Each Other

Always express love and respect for each other in marriage. It takes such a little time and so little effort to say, "I love you." Express appreciation. Show mutual respect. Sometimes we wonder why we forget it. Perhaps in marriage there may be a certain disregard for the other person's rights and opinions when we start to take them for granted. Let's not let this happen. Let's be good friends as well as sweethearts. Let us keep this expression of love and respect always in our hearts, in our words, in our voices, and in our actions. This is one of the pillars of a happy marriage.

Pray Together

Probably the most important step of all is to PRAY TOGETHER. *"The family that prays together, stays together."* All of us partners in marriage need to remember the nearer we keep to God, the nearer we draw to each other. When we cannot solve the many problems that arise — and who can? — we take them to the Infinite Healing Presence in prayer. And what is more important than coming to God with prayer, not only when we are in trouble but when we plan our work each day. We call this *praying ahead,* as we think of the day's activities and register them in Divine Mind. We call it also a *sharing prayer,* as we get our minds in order with a simple, quiet family prayer together in the morning.

Quietly now we think of these things as we prepare for our meditation.

Meditation

We give thanks for this day. We give thanks for the beauty, the love, and the joy of it. We give thanks for the opportunity of it. We give thanks for the peace that passes all understanding, that flows through our hearts and minds today. We are in order taday. We have an inner discipline and an inner balance which flow out into our lives. This harmony is expressed in our outer experiences. Our every action is filled with meaning and beauty all day long. And so it is.

6

How to Overcome Loneliness

HERE ARE five important steps that will relieve loneliness:

Number One: TAKE AN INTEREST IN YOUR WORLD

Number Two: LEARN TO LIKE PEOPLE

Number Three: LIVE YOUR LIFE FULLY

Number Four: CHOOSE YOUR GOALS AND STICK TO THEM

Number Five: GIVE SOMETHING OF YOUR-SELF EVERY DAY

Take an Interest in Your World

One of the worst diseases of mankind is boredom: this withdrawn, egocentric self-centeredness which keeps us from appreciating and understanding the things that go on about us. The world is really a wonderful place. Look about you and you see this beauty everywhere.

Sometimes people say, "Oh, I get tired of the world. Everything seems to be going so rapidly; there's so much struggle and stress and strain." We won't feel this way if we learn some things about living. Look around and see what your world is like. Everything is interesting because everything has come from ideas; everything has come from thoughts. The great natural beauty of the world, of course, has come from the thoughts which are known in the Infinite Mind of the universe. And what a Mind this must be!

Have you looked into the heart of a rose recently? Have you held it in your hand? Have you smelled its fragrance? Have you touched its velvety texture? Have you seen the intricacies of its patterns? Now pick up an artificial flower and look at it. It may be beautiful, may even have the fragrance of a rose. It may look and feel like a rose. But it can never duplicate the great natural beauty which has come straight from the mind and the heart of the Infinite Intelligence.

Look about you and see what a wonderful world it is! Pick up a seed, any kind of seed, and meditate for awhile upon the life that is contained in it: the great process which works automatically when we leave it alone and let it grow. The air that we breathe — the great space in which we move — the earth, which has the teeming nourishment and vibration of life itself — are some of the wonders of our world. It is good to understand and appreciate them.

Learn to Like People

Don Blanding used to tell of his old Aunt Calley, who said, "We better get used to like'n people, because they's the things that there's the most of." We need to get along with each other. We start by learning the principle of love: the great lesson that we are all children of the One Power; that we are all here endeavoring to do the best we can. Some of us are a little objectionable once in a while; but this will be overlooked and forgiven by our friends, if we are sincere in our efforts to express love and good will.

You will like people when you see that everyone is doing the best he can at the moment. Sometimes you may think this is not very good. But it is the best that he can do at that time; and if we understand him and encourage him because we like him, then he's going to be able to do better. He is going to "arrive," and we shall all have a real sense of accomplishment because we have helped him.

Strangely enough, it is easier to like other people when we like ourselves. If we accept ourselves as people of worth and dignity—as likeable, responsive people—we will find that we are liking other people better. The image that we hold of ourselves is important. *Each of us is a unique, wonderful individual, with a special contribution to make to life.* It is good to think of ourselves in that way, and then to remember that other people are just as wonderful.

Everyone likes to be appreciated—to be part of the life about him. Nothing is more pitiful than the person who feels that he is rejected, who feels that he is not wanted, who is shut out of things. We can break that feeling right now for ourselves and for other people if we will say honestly: *"Everything that comes from me expresses love and kindness and understanding. I love life, and I love to live. I like people, and I like to get along with them."* When we think thoughts like these each day, we can see how they change our attitude toward life and help to overcome loneliness.

Live Your Life Fully

As we said earlier, boredom is a terrible thing. Get out and get started today; get interested in something. Live your life fully. Take on a task: Go down to one of the charitable organizations or to a hospital, and volunteer to give some work. Get out and enjoy the things that are to be enjoyed; work at the things that need to be accomplished; read and study; travel a little bit; seek some worthwhile diversion; take up some sport.

Whatever your situation may be, you need to know the importance of learning to live your life fully. Get interested in a hobby, in a craft of some kind. Sit down and write a good letter; or sit down and write a short story. Try your hand at a poem. Go down to the beach and walk along, breathing in the freshness of the ozone. Go out and take a sun-bath, and let the rays of the warming sun penetrate deep within you. You will live more fully today if you do some of these things.

Choose Your Goals and Stick to Them

How important this step is! The loneliest kind of life is one without meaning or purpose. A good life cannot be lived without goals, without ideals, without purpose. Choose these carefully. Who are you? Where are you going? What do you want to be? What do you want to do? What do you want to give? What are your abilities? Choose a reasonable goal; then say, *"I am this thing: I am a good secretary, or I am a good businessman. I'm a good salesman. I'm a good clerk. I have a deep desire and an ambition to do these things. I am willing to learn the skills and develop the attitudes needed to succeed."*

Then bless your work today. If you do not like

it, doubly bless it. As you praise your work, it becomes possible for you to grow into a job which may suit you better. But you must *keep ever before you and within you the goal that you are striving for.* Keep alive in your mind the image of the work you really want to do, and prepare for it in every way you can.

While enthusiasm and interest in your work cannot take the place of warm, friendly human relations, such feelings can greatly enrich your life. You always have something to do to fill vacant hours. Out of such interests, friendships often grow. And because of your interest and enthusiasm, you yourself become a more interesting person.

Give Something of Yourself Each day

It is not enough to give money, to give things, or to give time. We must give of ourselves cheerfully, gladly, with a smile. There is a need for every one of us or we would not be here. The best way we can repay the great gift of life is to give of ourselves, to help other people, and to help make the world a better place in which to live.

Mrs. Harrison, a woman in her seventies, was the kind of person who lived this philosophy. A friend said of her one day, "Mrs. Harrison always makes me think she is especially glad to see me. She has such a warm, friendly greeting."

A young woman standing nearby overheard the

remark. "Isn't it strange?" she said. "I always thought Mrs. Harrison liked me especially well. *That's the way she makes me feel.*"

Mrs. Harrison was never without friends. She gave something of herself each day: the warmth and cordiality of one who understands and accepts people as they are. This is perhaps the truest way we can give of ourselves.

We have talked about five steps for overcoming loneliness:

TAKE AN INTEREST IN YOUR WORLD

LEARN TO LIKE PEOPLE

LIVE YOUR LIFE FULLY

CHOOSE YOUR GOALS AND STICK TO THEM

GIVE SOMETHING OF YOURSELF EACH DAY

Read each section again. Make a list of the suggestions that appeal to you. Then follow through with action. In this way you can overcome loneliness and increase happiness in everyday living.

Meditation

Let us be still and know this, each one about himself. Today I love life, and I love to live. I look about my world. I am interested in it. I see great beauty there. I love the people in it, and I give the best of myself to them and to everything that I do. Today I am living my life fully. I have noble goals, ambitions and ideals. I choose these wisely and I stick to them. As I give of myself to life, I know that life is giving itself to me. I give thanks that this is so. And so it is.

7

Five Steps to Prosperity

THESE FIVE steps to prosperity can be simply stated:

Number One: KNOW THAT GOD IS THE SOURCE OF YOUR SUPPLY

Number Two: KNOW THAT THERE IS NO LACK IN THE UNIVERSE

Number Three: RID YOUR MIND OF LIMITATION

Number Four: KNOW THAT GOD CANNOT SAY NO

Number Five: DECIDE WHAT YOU WANT AND ACCEPT IT

God Is the Source of Your Supply

What does it mean when we say that GOD is the source of our supply? What is God, anyway? God means the All Good, the great universal Power and Intelligence. Stop for a moment right now, and think in terms of a Power greater than you are. Think of the magnificence of life, of the great universe spreading out before you, of all the abundance which is being expressed everywhere. Then know that *the same Power which has created this rich outpouring of life is producing abundance through all of us right now.* It is giving us the food we eat, the water we drink, the air we breathe, the money we spend, the clothes we wear, the houses in which we live, the cars we drive.

Let us give thanks for these things right now. We do not need to get on our knees or make any particular ceremony out of our thanksgiving. Let's just say, *"Thank you, Father, for the abundance which is mine."* All things flow from this quiet center where God lives in our hearts. God is the All Good, the Universal Power of Life—not a person, but very personal to each of us as we become aware of the Presence within.

GOD IS THE SOURCE OF OUR SUPPLY. If we take this thought into our minds today, caress it and bless it and praise it, it will change our lives from this moment forward. We are not dependent on people or things for our good. God alone is the source of our supply. Like a great reservoir upon which we draw, a great bank account upon which we write checks, this Source is always there. Our supply comes to us through the channels of our jobs, sometimes through unexpected sources. But the first step toward prosperity of any kind is to recognize that God is the source of our supply.

There Is No Lack in the Universe

There is no lack in the universe. Look around your yard at home. You see the grass growing, you see the flowers, you see the leaves on the trees. There is no lack there. Plants and trees draw their nourishment from the soil and from the air. There is no lack there.

Walk outside and look into the sky. You see the abundance which is there: air, clouds, sky—the blue which stretches into outer space—no lack anywhere! Drive out into the country and see the various kinds of plants and flowers, shrubs and trees growing in abundance. In addition, there are billions and billions of seeds, nestling there on the earth awaiting their call to grow. No lack anywhere!

Perhaps you have been to the beach lately! You may have scooped up sand in your hands, letting it flow through your fingers and feeling its abundance. Think of the infinite number of grains of sand on beaches throughout the world. Look out at the ocean. Think of the inifinite number of buckets of water that are there! There is no lack in the universe. There is abundance everywhere.

These first two steps toward prosperity, then, are clear — knowing that GOD IS THE SOURCE OF OUR SUPPLY and that THERE IS NO LACK IN THE UNIVERSE. Now we are ready to go the next step.

Rid Your Mind of Limitation

If there is any limitation or fear, it exists in our own minds. *There is no lack in the universe.* As we get a sense of abundance, as we learn to treat and pray effectively, as we learn to think constructively and act creatively, the limitations disappear.

Limitation is a fear of lack, and it exists first in our own minds. It is important that we rid ourselves of thoughts of limitation so that the law of abundance can operate through our affairs. If we are experiencing lack of any kind — lack of health, lack of work, lack of money, lack of companionship — we know that this limitation and the fear of it were first present in our minds. Getting rid of the fear and the thought of limitation is one of the important steps toward enjoying the plenty of the universe. We do this by saturating our minds with thoughts of the abundance everywhere about us.

God Cannot Say No

God as law, the great law of right action, cannot say NO. People pray to God. They ask for things and sometimes they don't get them. They say that God has said *no,* but God cannot say *no.* We say NO to OURSELVES when we are unhappy, when we are suspicious, when we are fearful. When we are doubtful, when we resent and hate other people, we are saying *no* to life. God as law, cannot say YES to you and NO to me. The law plays no favorites, but acts according to Principle. It always says YES, because *the will of God is the will of life.* It is we who all too often say *no* to ourselves. When we learn to pray with the affirmative consciousness of life flowing through us, then we have abundance expressing itself in our lives at all times according to our need.

Decide What You Want and Accept It

It is said that God provides food for every bird, but He doesn't go about and drop it into each nest. God is the source of supply, but we need to decide what we want. We can consciously create circumstances by making our choices. Decide what it is you want today. Do you want to be a better person? Do you want a finer life for yourself and your family? Do you want a better job? Do you want a larger income? Do you want more peace, harmony and beauty? Do you want better health?

Decide what it is that will be the truest expression of yourself. You are entitled to it. Accept it and know that it is yours. But know, too, that God can give us only that which we ARE. *Each of us must build in his heart and mind the mental equivalent of that which he wants.* God works as law and as love. Life demands that we fulfill the law, but love multiplies many times the efforts which we make.

If you would be prosperous then:

KNOW THAT GOD IS THE SOURCE OF
   YOUR SUPPLY

KNOW THAT THERE IS NO LACK IN
   THE UNIVERSE

RID YOUR MIND OF LIMITATIONS

KNOW THAT GOD CANNOT SAY NO

KNOW WHAT YOU WANT AND
   ACCEPT IT

Meditation

Let us be still and accept complete prosperity in all of our affairs. We accept the free, full flow of abundance which is taking place through us, through our families and friends right now. We praise the great Source of all good. We praise God from whom all blessings flow. We know there is no lack anywhere, and we accept the abundance which is now flowing into our minds and hearts. This universe is spilling out its blessings for us today, and we accept them with gratitude and with great joy. And so it is!

8

How to Meet Trouble

EVERYONE HAS trouble or problems at some time in his life, so it behooves us to adopt a WAY OF LIFE that will enable us to meet trouble courageously and creatively. Here are a few suggestions that will help:

Number One: WHERE THE TROUBLE
              SEEMS TO BE, GOD IS
              ALREADY THERE

Number Two: YOU CAN HANDLE YOUR
              PROBLEM

Number Three: GIVE THANKS FOR GOOD

Number Four: GATHER YOUR FORCES
              AND ACT

Where the Trouble Seems to Be, God Is Already There

Reaffirm your faith in the eternal goodness of God by accepting the idea that where the trouble seems to be, God is already there. Oh, it is easy to say, isn't it?—but much more difficult to practice. We should start where we are, however, and it is unthinkable that we can start anywhere except in cooperation with that loving perfect Power which is greater than we are.

We see trouble and problems about us at all times. People have personal tragedies. Insurmountable difficulties seem to arise. A person may seem to have everything going just about right when here comes "Old Man Trouble." He upsets the apple cart, and a person has a difficult time keeping his life on an even keel.

The first step, then, is important. Realize that WHERE THIS TROUBLE SEEMS TO BE, GOD IS ALREADY THERE. Can you think of trouble as an illusion—*as nothing trying to be something?* Oh yes, it is real in ONE sense. *Trouble is FACTUAL in your experience when it comes, but it is not REALITY*.

We can never see the full truth of any situation. We can only feel the spiritual force of evolution which operates on many planes and which is ever moving us along to greater expression of ourselves. In the trouble that we face, there may be the opportunity to gather greater strength — to learn our greatest lesson.

It is hard to know sometimes WHY trouble comes to us. But we do know from our study of TRUTH *that there is a law of cause and effect which flows through all things.* This law operates on many levels, some of which we do not understand. There may be an inner need or destiny that we have not sensed. There may have been mistakes in thinking, or consistently negative attitudes which have caused certain things to come into our lives.

When trouble takes the form of the death of a dear one, these words may seem hardly adequate. But if we think in terms of the larger concept that THERE IS NO DEATH, we come to know that death itself can be a most creative experience for all concerned. We cannot always understand the destiny of our loved ones. We know there is no fatalism nor rigid plan back of life, but there is a great movement toward wholeness and productivity. How are we to know the way in which each life can be most productive?

You Can Handle Your Problem

A second help in time of trouble is to realize that WE SHALL NEVER BE CONFRONTED WITH A SITUATION OR PROBLEM WE ARE NOT CAPABLE OF HANDLING. We may feel that we have been flooded with challenges and with crises that we do not know how to handle. It is good to know that *we would never attract to ourselves those things unless we were equal to them.*

Our TRUE life is the life of God, which is an IN-VINCIBLE POWER. It knows how to do and to be all things. The mind that we use, the intelligence that we have, is our use of God's mind, the ONE MIND which knows all the answers. You can see the reason that we shall never be confronted with a problem we are not capable of handling.

The awareness of this PRESENCE within gives us strength. It gives us courage to go out into our world and to face trouble whatever it may be, be-cause *we are stronger than anything that can con-front us.* We should learn to judge according to this vital inner truth rather than by the appearances that assail us. *We are surrounded and indwelt by invin-cible strength.* Let us look at every problem from that viewpoint.

Give Thanks for Good

Our third step says: No matter what may happen, learn to say and to mean, "FATHER, I DO GIVE THEE THANKS FOR THIS EVIDENCE OF THY LOVE FOR ME." This may be difficult to do, but it is the *only* way. We must learn to give thanks for positive values. This helps to strengthen us within so that we may meet the problems and the troubles which assail us from the outside. *The pearl of great price, the secret of wisdom, is to know that the cause of all things proceeds from within outward. If we would have the strength to meet the outer situation, we must learn to build a "stately mansion" in the soul.*

We must learn to build a fiber of strength in our very being. Learn to say, *"Father, I do give thanks for the good from this experience as evidence of Thy love for me."* This realization is a great step in surrendering the hurt and the resentment and the defensiveness of the little personal ego. Then the great power, which is God's Infinite Intelligence and Presence within us, can help us. We move into cooperation and into harmony with It by adopting an attitude of thanksgiving. No matter if it is a problem, if it is a hurt, if it is a loss, if it is a tragedy — *thank God for the good that comes from it.*

Remember, *you would never have been confronted with this situation unless you were capable of handling it.* The need for creative action releases tremendous powers and potentials within you. As our experiences unfold, faith helps us to see that they are part of a pattern of good constantly unfolding in our lives. Whatever happens — if it is good or if it is seemingly bad — if it is gay or if it is sad — we can use it to serve the kingdom. Learn to carry this state of mind, and it will help to change the entire tenor of your life.

Gather Your Forces and Act

The fourth step in meeting trouble is important. GATHER YOUR FORCES TOGETHER; PRACTICE AFFIRMATIVE PRAYER; DO WHAT YOU HAVE TO DO WITH COURAGE, FAITH AND STRENGTH. Whenever you are confronted with a problem or with trouble, practice affirmative prayer, recognizing the presence of God. Relate yourself to this Presence. See this Power flowing into and through every aspect of the problem. Use your God-given imagination to see clearly the positive results that can be achieved.

Then go out and do what needs to be done with courage, faith and strength. No one likes a whiner; no one likes a defeatist. Oh, we are entitled to lick our wounds occasionally, but we must eventually pull ourselves together. The one great challenge is LIFE itself. To live we must face life. To face it with courage and faith in a HIGHER POWER releases powers within us which enable us to meet every situation, whatever it may be. We have the strength that we need, the vitality, the uprightness and the resiliency that make for good living. Let us keep a constant awareness of the Presence within. This will give us inner strength. It will instruct and guide us, not only in how to meet trouble but in how to move forward into a realization of the GREATER SELF.

Meditation

Let us be still and go forward into our world, bolstered and strengthened with an indwelling consciousness of peace, order and vitality. We have faith in a HIGHER POWER. We learn to say, "Where the problem seems to be, God is already there." We realize that the thanksgiving which we give for all of life covers everything that could possibly happen. We go forward into our world with courage, faith and strength. We are surrounded and indwelt by the great Healing Presence of the Universe. And so it is.

9

How to Get the Most Out of Life

THERE ARE four major points that lead to happiness in everyday living. They are simple:

Number One: PLANNING

Number Two: DOING

Number Three: RELEASING

Number Four: ENJOYING

Planning

What have you done about this day? Did you sit down at the breakfast table and talk it over with your family? How much planning have you done? You should be the architect making the blueprints from which each day's experiences are to be built.

Take time to think through in your imagination the kinds of experiences you want.

Planning is important at many levels: planning the moment, planning the hour, planning the day, planning the week, planning the month, planning the year, planning one's life. This is a natural time sequence which leads to the steady unfoldment of life's experiences.

The importance of planning, with flexibility for changing circumstances, cannot be over-estimated. How could we expect to achieve worthy goals and ambitions unless we plan what we want to do? If, for example, you went to the bank, presented a check at the cashier's window, and said, "Give me some money, please," he would reply, "Make out the specific amount you want, and I shall be glad to give it to you if you have it in the bank."

But if you say, "Oh, just give me enough for weekly expenses," he would say, "I'm sorry, but you have to write on the check the exact amount you want."

Life is like that. It is up to us to be specific, to be definite. Remember *man's job is WHAT; God's job is HOW.* God knows how to fulfill our desires if we know WHAT it is we want. The law cannot say NO. It cannot withhold anything that belongs to us. It simply says, "Use your power of initiative. Choose what you want and develop the mental equivalent of it in your mind." This power of choice is one of the most important attributes that have ever been given to man.

So learn to plan each day. One of the best ways to do this is to work through the day in your mind. Decide the different things you hope to accomplish during the day. Not too many, because you may not finish them all. This is frustrating to the inner man and develops a bind, a tension—a pressure.

Think about your plans this way: What are you going to do with your morning? Do you have work to do at home? Are you working on a creative project? Do you have some business deals on at the office? Then what are you going to do this afternoon? Do you have some errands to do, some shopping, some calls that you have been putting off, some letters to write, some interviews or appointments to set up? Whatever you want to do, think about it during your planning time.

Then what are you going to do in the evening? Are you going to continue in business relationships, or will it be a social evening? Perhaps it is an evening at home in which you improve your mind and your soul and enjoy your family. Whatever it is, be specific about your plans.

Allow for some fluctuation and some flexibility, but in general plan your day as specifically as possible. Then say,

> *I know that the power of the Infinite Mind indwells me and goes before me preparing the way. It gives me strength. It gives me whatever I need to fulfill these objectives. I give thanks for a day perfectly planned. I*

now release this into the law of creative action, and I give thanks that this day is an already completed unit of time and experience in the Infinite Mind.

That is the treatment; that is planning ahead. It has been called rather jokingly, "PRAYING AHEAD," and it is a good idea. Don't pray just when you are in trouble or when you want to get something. Plan your day with prayer. Prayer is not a theological term; it is talking to God. *Talk to God about your day.* Plan it, and watch it unfold.

Doing

Then we come to the second step, which is DOING. I have spent a good deal of time discussing PLAN-NING because the preparation which goes into any project is the most important part of it. You wouldn't start building a house by putting on the roof first; so don't plan a day or a lifetime by trying to do the last things first. We should start at the beginning and PLAN our activities.

But inevitably in any sequence of the creative process the time comes for DOING. After you have planned your day, you get up from the breakfast table, or arrive at your office, and you ACT. You tackle "the thing that couldn't be done" and you do it — that's all.

Now the things that you have planned must be

done in order. Plan the things to do first and start right in. Start in on that desk if that is part of your plan. Clear the mail. Answer it. If there is a letter that you can't answer, put it at the bottom of the pile. Go ahead dictating, typing or whatever you are doing. When next you come to this letter, look at it, plan what you want to say, what you want to do with it. Maybe the temptation is to say, "Well, we'll let that go," but when you have to answer it, think about it and then act. This will keep the channel clear. Doing things in proper order will make for relaxation and health as well as greater success and happiness. PLAN, then ACT!

Releasing

RELEASING is the third step in getting the most out of life. Here is a step that we have to think about for a moment. Releasing means to let go. When you have planned, when you have done all the work you can, then release your project and let it happen.

Many of us are engaged in building organizations or businesses, in working with numbers of other people. Sometimes we try to make things happen; but we discover — don't we? — that we cannot *make* anything happen. After prayer and proper action we must turn it over to God and LET it happen.

The great George Washington Carver said that early in his career as a scientist, he picked up a peanut and held it in his hand. He was a very devout man, and he prayed, "Please, God, tell me about this peanut." And the Lord answered, "You have a mind of your own. Go and find out."

Carver was wise enough to release his project to Divine Intelligence. Every morning he went out into the open and talked to GOD ABOUT HIS WORK. He was wise enough also to use his own mind and to work patiently and serenely. As a result, he found over three hundred uses for the peanut.

It is a wonderful thing to plan, to work, and then to let go and get ourselves out of the way so Divine Law can operate.

Enjoying

The final step is ENJOYING. Enjoy what you plan. Enjoy what you do. Enjoy watching your plans unfold after you have released them into the mind of God. Live each moment happily and abundantly. Seek out the kinds of experiences that you enjoy — the kind of recreation that stimulates and invigorates you. Enjoy realization as part of the rhythm of life.

Be keenly aware of your surroundings, responsive to people and to situations. Be joyous and grateful for the good that is yours. Our life today is part of eternity. Enjoy it now.

Meditation

Quietly now we turn to the Infinite Power within, to that great Creative Principle which takes our plans and brings them to fruition. Fear is transformed into courage and confidence, for we know that our plans are God's plans. We do the work that needs to be done, then release our plans to the Infinite Creative Law. We enjoy watching our plans unfold. We give thanks for all the blessings Life has brought us and for the laws of fulfillment which we have learned. And so it is.

10

The Power of Faith

THE POWER of faith is tremendous. But faith, like happiness, is hard to define. Perhaps Paul came closest to a definition when he said: *"Now faith is the substance of things hoped for, the evidence of things not seen."* Notice that he says FAITH is SUBSTANCE. It is something real and tangible. It is an inner mental and emotional conviction, the evidence of things not seen. Paul also said, *". . . things which are seen were not made of things which do appear."* The things which we see are made of inner conviction, the state of consciousness which we hold, the faith that we have. Ernest Holmes said that faith is a mental conviction that cannot conceive of its opposite.

In our everyday living four kinds of faith are important:

Number One: FAITH IN OURSELVES AND
                         OTHERS

Number Two: FAITH IN OUR COUNTRY
               AND OUR WAY OF LIFE

Number Three: FAITH IN THE TRIUMPH
               OF GOOD OVER EVIL

Number Four: FAITH IN GOD

Faith in Ourselves and Others

How do you usually think of yourself? Are you weak or are you strong? Are you sick or healthy? Are you limited or are you prosperous? Whatever you think now, let us build faith in constructive ideas. Build up the faith, the inner conviction that whatever you need to do, you can do. There is a Power within you equal to any situation. God is your partner. This faith is a way of life. It is strong, vital, dynamic. If we have faith, this faith will attract to us that which we need. Do you have faith in your talent? Do you have faith in your mental processes? Do you have faith in your ability? Do you have faith in that Power within? If you do, you will believe in your capacity to do whatever it is that you need to do today.

What is your day presenting to you? Is it just another day with drawn-out, humdrum, routine tasks? All right, let us have faith in our capacity to make it something different. Let's try to do old things in a new way today. Let's say right now:

*I have faith that this day is now the best day
that I have ever had. I don't know what's*

ahead for me, but I have faith that it will be good, because I have faith in myself; I have faith in my abilities. I know that whatever I need is already at hand and finds its way to me. I know that I am recognized, that my work is appreciated.

We are treating ourselves right here and now — aren't we? — to have greater faith in ourselves. Believe in yourself, because YOU ARE A WONDER-FUL PERSON. You are an open channel through which all the good, all the abundance and all the power, all the beauty and joy and wonderful things of life flow. Believe this and it opens your mind; it uplifts your heart; it enlivens your consciousness. Faith is a tremendous dynamic. Just having faith in the presence of an Infinite Power is enough to give you health. Faith in the flow of abundance causes the good things of life to flow into your experience.

Faith in our fellow men is important, as well as faith in ourselves. Do you like the people around you? Do you like what they are trying to do? Do you like the people in your office, the people in your family? Do you like your friends, your neighbors, your casual acquaintances and contacts? Do you see every person as an individualized expression of God? Let's adopt an attitude of faith in people. Let's tell them we have faith in them. If you are a supervisor, or have charge of a number of people, let them know that you believe in them. Praise them a little. Tell them you appreciate what they are doing. If they are having difficulty, tell them that you understand. A little word of faith and encouragement in the morning when you first get to the office, or your place of business, will do wonders in bringing increased dividends in human relations and in outer tangible effects.

Faith in Our Country

Have faith in our country and in our way of life. Don't you love this wonderful United States of ours? Our forefathers had great vision. They had faith that there could be founded on this earth a government dedicated to the proposition *"that all men are created equal; that they are endowed by their Creator with certain inalienable rights; that among these are life, liberty, and the pursuit of happiness."* Have faith in this ideal. Have faith in this dream; back it up in every way.

Let's stop complaining about taxes, the bunch in Washington, the criticism of such things as the smog and the traffic. Let's concentrate on building our own faith. Let us pick our country as an object of our faith. Let us praise it and bless it so that it may come to full bloom. We are a young country; we are in the growing stage. Did you ever see a perfect adolescent? Naturally our country is not perfect as yet; but our way of life offers great blessings and will achieve more as the years go by. I am talking about the ideal now. A lot of things we see are far from perfect. You can't have faith in some of the nonsense that goes on, but griping about it is not going to change it. *Have faith in an Indwelling Presence and a constantly available intelligence which we can use to improve things.*

Faith in the Triumph of Good

Do you have faith in the triumph of good over evil? Here is the test: *Do you honestly believe in the power of the mind? Do you honestly believe we can change conditions through prayer and treatment? Do you believe that faith gives us power?* Jesus said, "Resist not evil," implying that we should overcome evil with good. We should have faith that good will win out.

But you say, "Well, I don't think so; I read the papers, and I can see what's going on around me." Conditions were the same in the time of Jesus. Because many people believed in evil, Jesus said, ". . . men loved darkness rather than light . . ." But people prefer the light when they have learned to overcome evil with good. To do this, *each of us as individuals, and all of us as mankind, must learn to think, feel, speak and act from the Center of good at the heart of each of us.* Believe in this good. Know that it is ever available, ever working, ever unfolding, ever waiting to be expressed. Put faith in good in your heart today and watch what happens.

Faith in God

All through this discussion we have touched on the importance of faith in God, the Universal Presence and Power which indwells each of us. *Faith in God is the single most vital, important force in our lives.* Having faith in this mighty Power greater than we are brings a deep, underlying sense of "peace that passeth all understanding." This is a basic part of happiness and success in everyday living.

As our faith in God increases, we look out upon the world with enthusiasm, expectation, and faith that good is unfolding in our lives. We do not know what's ahead, but it can only be good. As our faith in God increases, we find the gateway to the true self, thereby opening ourselves to the experience of richer, fuller living.

Meditation

Let us be still and accept this deep, strong, vital, challenging, creating, living faith. We have faith today in good. We know that good in our hearts triumphs over all worry, all mistakes, all problems of every kind. God is our strength. The great Law of the universe flowing through this Infinite Intelligence which we know as God is creating through us now a glorious, beautiful and wonderful life. And so it is.

11

Guides to Spiritual Understanding

I. The Nature of God

GOD IS Infinite. God is Spirit. No man can comprehend this Spirit in Its fullness, yet It is personal and responsive to each individual. God is Spirit — both Presence and Principle, individualizing as the Divine Spark within each of us, the gift of God to every man.

God can be described in many ways: First Cause, the great Creative Principle of the universe, the Infinite Healing Presence.

Troward gives the attributes of God as *Life, Love, Light, Power, Peace, Beauty* and *Joy.* Perhaps the words we use do not matter too much. It is important that God become real to us through experience of the Divine Presence within.

II. The Nature of Man

Man is created in the "image and likeness of God." He is a personalized expression of the UNI-VERSAL, consisting of spirit, mind and body. The great Creative Principle of the universe, acting through laws on many planes, creates the environment in which man lives. The Infinite Healing Presence within man is constantly leading him toward greater expression of wholeness. Man has the power to choose the kind of life through which he can best express his true self.

III. The Relationship of God and Man

God is the the invisible partner with every man in every undertaking. Man has freedom to choose his goals. The Creative Law then works toward their accomplishment. It acts according to laws of its own; but it acts also in accord with the imagination, the thoughts, emotions, and deeds of the individual. God and man are one, yet each has his part to play in the drama of life.

IV. The Laws of the Universe

In the Kingdom of God, all things are known. The laws which scientists are discovering have always existed. It was only necessary that they be uncovered. So it is with laws on all planes: physical, mental, spiritual. As we grow in our consciousness of the Indwelling Presence, as we become more like It in our thoughts, feelings and deeds, we understand and act in accord with positive mental and spiritual laws. We come to know that love is the fulfilling of all law. Feelings of fear, hate, resentment, negative criticism and guilt are transformed into faith, love, forgiveness and appreciation. The energy of all these emotions is turned toward love and service for others.

Personal Treatment for Happiness

Today I am a happy person. I look upon life as a great opportunity to live. I learn, I grow and I work to express all that is beautiful and all that is good. My life is a time of great and glorious adventure. I do what is necessary to change, and I am happy to be alive. I am a happy person now. And so it is.

Personal Treatment for Success

I ACCEPT life with all its challenges and opportunities.

I EXPRESS life through an unbroken succession of unfolding experiences, and all are good.

I ENJOY life. I take an interest in every phase and particle of it that I possibly can, because life is completely wonderful and fascinating.

I LIVE life because it is infinitely worth living.

AND SO IT IS.

12

Daily Guides to Happiness
and Success

1

Today Is My Day, I Live It Fully
Every day will I bless thee.   *Psalm 145:2*

This day is God's gift to me and to all men. To-day I am immersed in new and tremendous experience. There is no limit to my accomplishment on this day because God is in action through me. Whatever I set my hand to is already done. God is the inspiration of my life and the strength of my being.

2

My Work Is Joyous Expression
The labourer is worthy of his hire.   *Luke 10:7*

My work is the channel through which I carry on my Father's business. I appreciate it; I love it; I bless it. I am worthy of my hire today because I am engaged in mighty projects. Nothing is too great for my capacities or too small for my attention. God expresses Himself through me. I am a joyous action of Creation today.

3

I Understand the Spiritual Reality of Life
The Spirit searcheth all things, yea, the deep things of God.   *1 Corinthians 2:10*

Today I know that there is a Reality within all Life which is greater than all things which appear. Never again do I judge by appearances. God has given me the gift of seeing the Truth. Nothing can discourage me. God is within all things. He alone is real. Everything I see is a picture of God.

4

Faith Abolishes Fear from My Consciousness
Let not your heart be troubled, neither let it be afraid.   *John 14:27*

Nothing unlike the Nature of God has residence in my consciousness. My perfect faith casts out all fear. I have faith in the Father because He has such complete faith in me. He knows that I am perfect in His image. The unfoldment of the Universe eternally repeats its infinite and immutable pattern through me. Today I have complete faith.

5

The Infinite Power within Me Knows No Limitation

The things which are impossible with men are possible with God.   Luke 18:27

As I breathe deeply of inspiration and realization, I know I am partaking of the Larger Reality. I now let go of all human restrictions and limitations. My creative consciousness is completely free. I feel myself one with all Being, and all trifling problems and matters disappear from my mind. I accept the Larger Reality of myself and the Creative Action of Mind manifests It for me.

6

Infinite Mind Eternal Flows through Me

Renew a right spirit within me.   Psalm 51:10

I am linked into a circuit of supply and power which never ceases its operation through me. My only responsibility is to keep this circuit open and allow it to express itself in terms of what it is — Perfect Expression. My every idea, thought or attitude throws the switch which completes the Divine Circuit. It flows for me as I flow with it.

7

I Am Charged with Limitless Energy
Come unto Me, all ye that labour and are heavy laden, and I will give you rest.   Matthew 11:28

Energy is thought being thought. The illumination which I draw from Universal Intelligence, and my response to it, determine the rate of vibration of my thinking. The vibrations which emanate from my individual use of the One Mind are expressions of Infinite energy. As I understand this principle I know that I am expressed from the original Source of all Being — Unconditioned Energy — Light — Mind.

8

I Claim the Fullness of Life Today
What things soever ye desire, when ye pray, believe that ye receive them, and ye shall have them.
Mark 11:24

My faith is the real measure of my capacity. There is no limitation in my consciousness except that which I place there through the repeated patterns of false thinking. Recognition of Infinite Good removes all blocks from my consciousness. I am an open channel for abundant Life expression. Today I deepen my concept of God and myself. The depth of my thinking releases larger experience for me.

9

I Am One with the Higher Intelligence

Trust in the Lord with all thine heart; and lean not unto thine own understanding.   Proverbs 3:5

Today I meditate upon the essential Unity of all existence and experience. Universal Life finds in me an outlet for Its expression. Infinite Mind thinks through me. I am an active and self-directed unit of the machinery of Life. My job is thinking, working, and living so that God is visibly expressed through me in terms of His own perfection.

10

The Abundance of Life Is Mine

I am come that they might have life, and that they might have it more abundantly.   John 10:10

Life is synonymous with abundance. Nature is the lavish expression of a Mind which knows no limitation. Creative Intelligence is free from restriction and does not withhold anything from Its creations. I cannot be deprived of anything which I recognize and claim as my own. Abundance of Spirit is my eternal supply. I am filled with it. I use it wisely.

11

The Infinite Desires My Success

If God be for us, who can be against us?
Romans 8:31

Success indicates that we are working in cooperation with the Creative Force. Conflict with it produces failure. I need no longer wonder if God wants me to have certain things. He wants me to have whatever is of good, of beauty, and of service. I eliminate from my thinking all belief in struggle and competition. All that the Father has is mine.

12

Consciousness Is My Inner Reality

The Kingdom of God is within you.   Luke 17:21

Today I discern the difference between that which is real and that which is unreal. There is a spiritual and mental equivalent behind all experience. Life is expressed from an inner reality. This inner factor is the sum total of all that I am. This is my consciousness. I am One with Him. I know Reality.

13

Superior Power Acts through Me

For God hath not given us the spirit of fear; but of power, and of love, and of a sound mind.

                                    II Timothy 1:7

There is only One Force. It works with all the Power there is to produce faithfully whatever is thought into It. The Law acts through me as a reaction to what I have directed It to do. Today I control myself and my thoughts. I think good, speak good, and expect only good to come to me today. "This is the day which the Lord hath made; we will rejoice and be glad in it."

14

Sound Judgment Governs My Activities

Thou shall guide me with thy counsel, and afterward receive me to glory.   *Psalm 73:24*

Judgment and discernment are tools of my mind. They enable me to steer a true course. I am careful not to dull their edges. I keep them sharp and bright by using them creatively. I learn to judge righteous judgment by discerning the cause behind conditions and circumstances. The appearance points the way to the lesson within. I learn this lesson. I use perfect judgment today.

15

I Cooperate with God Today

God is our refuge and strength, a very present help in trouble.   *Psalm 46:1*

It is folly to try to go it alone. Why should I try to push the automobile when the powerful engine under the hood is just waiting for me to switch on the ignition so that it may propel me along the road I wish to travel? From this moment I determine to cooperate witih the living God-engine within me. It does the work.

16

I am Attuned to Inner Guidance

Incline your ear, and come unto Me: hear, and your soul shall live.   *Isaiah 55:3*

I learn to listen. Within me is a Guiding Intelligence which is constantly inspiring and instructing me. The Voice speaks to me in the language of prayer, meditation, and contemplation—or sometimes as a hunch, or a "feeling." I depend upon this Inner Guidance and I follow Its directions. I have Faith in the Wisdom of the Father. My life is the action of Infinite Instruction.

17

Perfect and Complete Results
Are My Guarantee

Ask, and it shall be given you; seek, and ye shall find; knock, and it shall be opened unto you.

Matthew 7:7

God and man are signatories to a contract which always works. The terms of the Divine Compact are always in force. There is no margin for error in God's Scheme. As I love, I am loved. As I give, I receive. As I believe, it is realized through me. As I teach, I learn. As I think in my heart, so am I. Perfect balance is eternally maintained in my life.

18

There Is a Lesson in Every
Happening of This Day

I have learned, in whatsoever state I am, therewith to be content.   *Philippians 4:11*

I am here to learn by means of experience. Knowing this, I realize that there is great value in everything that takes place in my life. Everything that happens to me is the result of what I have thought and believed. I turn negative experiences into actions of good by learning from them. As I learn, I correct my thinking. My balanced consciousness is evidence of my progression.

19

I Live in Expectancy of Good

My soul, wait thou only upon God; for my expectation is from Him.   Psalm 62:5

I embody the expectancy of good today. My expectant attitude makes living a joyous adventure. All that the Father has is mine, and it is my destiny to experience all of it. Expectancy is Faith in action. An expectant mind is a receptive mind. I refuse to accept anything less than the best in any situation. I am my Father's son, and I expect to live so that He will be well pleased.

20

I Know What to Say, Think and Do

And the Lord shall guide thee continually.
Isaiah 58:11

My unity with Infinite Wisdom causes me to know what to say and think, and how to act. I let this guidance flow through me by letting go of all doubt, fear and belief in making mistakes. Thus,

Life expresses spontaneously, peacefully and harmoniously through me. My days are filled with unexpected happiness, friendly and appreciative associations, and smooth and easy action.

21

Each Day Is a New and Vital Experience

Be ye transformed by the renewing of your mind.
Romans 12:2

This is my day. It is my share of eternity in which I can experience anything which I wish. I can waste it or use it creatively. The choice is mine. I choose wisely now. I put my attention upon one task at a time and see it through to successful completion. I savor each moment and live it fully. I live in God's time.

22

My Works Are Accomplished
with Spiritual Power

But as many as received Him, to them gave He
power.   *John 1:12*

I am connected with God through the medium of spirit. There is One Mind and I am an individual action of It. I use It constantly. Therefore, I have limitless capacity and infinite power. There is no point at which I end and God begins. There is only One Action taking place through all Being. This is the Self-Projection of Creative Mind. I am evidence of It.

23

Inspiration Fills the Cup of Consciousness
If any man thirst, let him come unto Me, and drink.
                                            John 7:37

As soon as I am able to understand, I receive from within myself new thoughts, new ideas, and new challenges. My consciousness spirals upward in ever evolving development. My circumstances and conditions are always right. They are the inevitable consequence of my consciousness. My outer growth is evidence of inner Inspiration. Inspiration is the appearance of God at man's level. I am filled witih Inspiration today.

24

I Am Strong in All My Ways
I can do all things through Christ which strength-
eneth me.   *Philippians 4:13*

My strength is the amount of Creative Power which I call into action. Strength is faith applied to a specific task. Strength is the inbuilt mechanism of accomplishment. Strength is knowing how to use and be used by God. Strength results from right thinking. Strength is. I use it today. My strength is my knowing that the means are always available to do whatever needs to be done. I am strong.

25

I Am Part of the Larger Experience

In Him we live, and move, and have our being.
                                        Acts 17:28

Everything that has ever been thought, felt, said, or done is a part of what I am. I encompass all experience. I accept the larger viewpoint. I learn to blend my mind with the One Mind and let the Larger Thought flow through me. I am incapable of thinking of myself alone. My thought is a mosaic in the Infinite Pattern. I am One with Life.

26

My Soul Is Quiet and Untroubled

Thou wilt keep him in perfect peace, whose mind is stayed on Thee.   *Isaiah 26:3*

That which lives forever is not subject to temporal influence. As this truth becomes clear to me, I realize that my soul is actually independent of the forces and problems which seem to assail me. My soul is an eternal part of the One Soul. The serenity of the Universe is my true nature. Changeless and imperturbable is my individual divinity. All else is illusion. My soul is Reality incarnate within me.

27

I Talk with God Today

I sought the Lord, and He heard me, and delivered me from all my fears.   *Psalm 34:4*

Everything I say is putting into words what I think about God at that particular moment. Today I strive to make the words of my mouth acceptable in His sight. I consciously address myself to God until I pray without ceasing. I have a sense of Oneness in all that I do. As I talk with God, He talks to me. I listen. I learn. I act.

28

I Love My Fellowman

When ye stand praying, forgive, if you have ought against any.   *Mark 11:25*

A wish for my brother is actually a wish for myself. As I glory to the accomplishment and good fortune of others, I am actually sharing what they have received. This becomes true in my life when I understand Love. Love is my affirmative connection with Life and my fellowman. Love is uninhibited Creativity. Love is the true expression of living. I love today.

29

I am Charged with Infinite Power

This is the refreshing.   *Isaiah 28:12*

All fatigue and heaviness vanish from me as I pause and draw upon the infinite resources of Spirit. I receive living water as I drink deeply of the abundance of Infinite Intelligence. I am nourished by the action of Spirit. I return again and again to the Source. My life's batteries are eternally recharged there. I am connected with Life.

30

I Affirm My Oneness with God

Cast thy burden upon the Lord, and He shall sustain thee.   *Psalm 55:22*

Today the very stones sing out that God and Man are One. This is a very personal matter with me. God is all of me; I am part of Him. I pause in the day's occupation to grasp this tremendous truth.

Faith is born from my conviction, and fears and doubts are dissolved from my consciousness. Thank you, Father, for all that Life has to offer. I accept it as an expression of You.

31

Meditation Gives Me the Right Answer

They that wait upon the Lord shall renew their strength.   *Isaiah 40:31*

Each day I retire to the closet within and close the door. This is the secret place known only to God and me. It is the conference room where the plans and problems of Life are met. Nothing but Good emanates from this dwelling place of Infinite Spirit. I am at home there. I blend with all that is Universal. Thank you, Father, for hearing me.

Happiness & Success through Personal Power

Part II: Ten Steps

"How Can I . . . ?"

I N THE first five steps we discuss the power principles and their manifestations in your life. In the next five steps we construct the keys with which to unlock these personal powers in *your* life.

Most of us have asked, How can I get where I want to be? How can I get ahead faster? How can I get what I want from life? How can I become a success? How can I get results with my ideas? How can I make more money? How can I find more time to do the things I need to do? How can I find happiness? How can I establish security for myself and my family? How can I get some peace of mind? *HOW?*

The Ten Steps to personal power which are explained here provide the answers with which you can forge the keys that unlock the doors to health, happiness, prosperity, success and freedom. It works. Here we are providing you the answers, the knowledge which is the key to happiness and fulfillment. You can let that knowledge sit in your mental world and use it to daydream about all the things you will do—some day; *or.* . . . As with any key, it must be fitted into the lock and turned before the door will open.

Once you have become adept in its use you will find that the Ten Steps are the Master Keys to Success. Each of the Steps will fit many locks and open many doors—all leading to results which mean a richer, fuller life for you.*

Turn the Master Keys in the lock of your life today. No one else can do it for you. This technique for attaining Success is yours to use. It has worked for me. It will work for you. Use it.

---

*We are assuming that you have carefully studied the first part of this book, "Training."

You and Your Life

"**O** GOOD MASTER, how do I become great?" the student inquired of his teacher.

"By keeping eternally at it," the venerable sage replied, thus putting the responsibility for the student's life exactly where it belonged — with the student himself, the one who asked the question.

So it is with every one of us. No one can live for us. Whatever happens to us must happen through us. The success, power, happiness, health, riches or fame which we strive for are produced from our inner thoughts, feelings and attitudes. The potential of all things exists within us — the gift of life itself. It is up to each of us to give form and direction to this potential.

Every person has within himself the power to form the design of his own experience. When we realize this we have dominion over our world. Control, power and dominion are not achieved by our striving. They are the result of inner discipline, honesty, peace and follow-through.

"All things proceed from the quiet mind," says an ancient proverb.

"He who conquers a city is great; he who conquers himself is mighty," is a bit of timeless wisdom from the East.

In *Julius Caesar* Shakespeare admonishes:

> *The fault, dear Brutus,*
> *Lies not in our stars*
> *But in ourselves*
> *That we are underlings.*

We are not allowed the doubtful privilege of blaming others for our failures and shortcomings. Nor can we depend upon others to do for us that which we must do for ourselves. So face life. Live it. Develop the power within you and put it to work projecting the image of who you are and who you want to be. Get quiet inside, conquer the noisesome little self, assume responsibility for your own discipline and growth, establish honesty, firmness and integrity, and all power will be yours.

> *To thine own self be true*
> *And it must follow as the night the day*
> *Thou canst not then be false*
> *To any man.*
>
> Shakespeare, *Hamlet*

The desire to live properly and a determination to follow through are essential prerequisites as you follow the steps to power.

"How do I attain wisdom?" the student inquired of his teacher.

The sage turned away without answering.

"Please tell me how to be wise," begged the student.

The master silently walked away.

"I must have wisdom. Show me the way."

Arriving at the bank of the river, the teacher walked out into the water with the student in full pursuit.

"Wisdom, O great one! Show me how to become wise!"

Suddenly the master turned, grabbed the student's neck and held his head under water, keeping it there while the struggles became feebler and feebler. When the student had almost stopped striving, the teacher brought him gasping to the surface.

"When you were struggling beneath the surface, what did you want more than anything else in the world?" the master demanded.

"Air—air—!"

"Of course. And so it is with wisdom. When you desire it more than anything else—as much as you wanted air when you were drowning—then you will find it. But don't expect anyone else to tell you how to become wise. No one can do that, any more than they can breathe for you."

And so it is with the development of personal power—the inner power that leads to the rich, full life where there is a balance of happiness, health, prosperity, freedom and creative expression. We must be willing to perfect the inner causes which will make the outer results possible.

These are the tools to start with:

1. Faith in a Higher Power
2. Confidence in Yourself
3. Lively Interest in Everything and Everybody
4. Mastery of One Field of Endeavor
5. Dedication to Ideal and Purpose

"You Are the Power"

Do things happen when you get going? Are your plans working out? Are you able to get your work done on schedule? Do you have a feeling of accomplishment? Are you getting somewhere in life?

Right now is the time for personal inventory. Do your answers to the above questions show that you are living up to your full potential, or do they indicate a breakdown in the power circuits? The power is within you. In fact, YOU ARE THE POWER. The power doesn't have to be created, generated or injected into you from outside. There is no limit to the power available to you, because you are one with all the power there is. This is the secret of the ages — the pearl of great price. Start from here. Condition your mind to accept the conviction of invincible power. Follow this procedure:

1. Know that you are one with all the power there is.
2. Learn how to contact this power within you.
3. Learn how to cooperate with this power.
4. Learn how to use this power wisely.
5. Keep the power flowing.

Nothing is impossible to the person who lives by these principles. Life is energy. Everything is an expression of life-energy. We can either use it constructively or destructively. The power works both ways. It is up to us to decide how we are going to use it. When you use your personal power constructively, you will be in proper relationship to God, life, yourself, other people, your work. This relationship will produce an abundance of all good things in your life — happiness, health, prosperity, harmony and freedom. But when you use your personal power destructively, you are separated from healthy relationships, and are therefore shut off from the natural rewards of constructive living.

Now, no one deliberately sets out to destroy himself. No one knowingly turns his power to destructive uses. No one dissipates his life's energy on purpose. All of these things happen because we don't understand ourselves and the great natural laws under which we live. Therefore, mostly by omission rather than commission, we use our power against ourselves rather than to accomplish what we are here to do.

Part II of this book helps to remedy this situation by showing you how to know yourself on the five major levels of consciousness and experience — Spiritual, Mental, Emotional, Physical, Material — and how to put to use the five keys for manifestation in your life: Organize, Visualize, Energize, Realize, Actualize. These are your Ten Steps to personal power.

Spiritual Power

S PIRIT IS the source of all things. It is a perfectly good, practical, scientific word quite apart from anything mystical, metaphysical or theological. Let's learn to understand spirit and use it as our first step to personal power.

What do we mean when we say, "That fellow has a lot of spirit in him," or "That is a very spirited animal"? We are talking about life, aren't we? Of course. That is what spirit is. Life. Spiritual power is life power. Life must be lived. Spirit must be used. Actually, spirit is God within us. It is the eternal, enduring part. Spirit is what we really are—the higher self.

Spirit includes everything else; that's why we start with it. Spirit has been defined as "the power that knows itself." Real though it is, perhaps it cannot be fully explained. But the more we understand, the more we will know, and the more we know, the more power we have — spiritual power, with which we do things, and out of which we make things.

Spirit is the breath of life, infused into us from nature itself. The Greek word *pneuma,* the Latin word *spiritus,* and the Sanskrit word *prana,* are all used interchangeably to mean both "spirit" and "breath." When we inhale or "breathe in," we "inspire"; when we exhale or "breathe out," we "expire." *Expire* is also used when a person dies — when the spirit leaves the body.

You can readily see how the development of spiritual power must be our first step. When we have true spiritual power, all the rest will automatically follow.

There are ten steps to personal power, of which spiritual power is the first, and there are five steps to spiritual power:

1. *UNITY.* Become one with the source of all power.

2. *VISION.* Learn to see the larger scope of things.

3. *DEVOTION.* Love, praise and worship the wonder of life.

4. *JOY.* Let the magnificence and beauty of life fill you to overflowing.

5. *RELEASE.* Let the unobstructed flow of life fill you and work through you.

Unity

There is no place where God leaves off and you begin, and vice versa. You are a cell in the great spirit, the great mind and the great body of the universe. There is only ONE, and you are one with it. In unity there is strength. Strength is the basis of power. Separation weakens. All thought, feeling and action emanate from and return to the center of inner spiritual awareness. This center is the source of life — the source of power. Become aware of this magnificent potential within yourself. Don't even try to do anything yourself. Let spiritual power do it through you. Jesus said, "The Father that dwelleth in me, He doeth the works."

Vision

How far can you see? That is how far you can go. Each horizon is but the springboard for new goals, the taking-off place for new accomplishments. Develop unlimited vision. Probe into the meaning of things. Discern the causes back of all phenomena. Look past the error. See through to the Truth. Extend the range of your sight. Broaden your viewpoint. Get the larger picture. Contemplate the facts of life from the highest point of view. Remove the obstruction from your eye and you will see everyone and everything differently. Look into the distance.

See as far as you can. New vistas are beckoning. "If therefore thine eye be single, thy whole body shall be full of light."

Devotion

Spiritual power is the direct result of our worship. Worship is the process of loving, praising and blessing the oneness which is God. Call it by any name, but devote your inner attention to it. Contact and unify with the higher self—the spirit within you. Fall in love with the infinite goodness and give your entire self to it. Surrender completely. Give thanks to the source from which all things come. Praise the creative power which produces all things. Adore the very idea of life. Devote yourself to serving the good, the true and the beautiful.

Joy

Sing your praises from the hilltops. Let joy be unrestrained. It is great to be alive! Exultantly proclaim the good news. Let the vital surge of divine energy fill you to overflowing. Have a good time doing what you are doing. Life is a game. Have fun playing it. Let your laughter ring out. Bubble—sparkle—scintillate! Overflow with good will. Get interested in everything and everyone. Join the party.

Life is a ball! Let your excitement, interest and enthusiasm color everything you do. Infect others with your joyousness. Let your life be set to music. Love life and love to live it. Joyously greet each day. Joyously perform each task.

Release

Effort, struggle, strain and concern must go. Why should you wear yourself out when there is a better way? You ARE the power, and the power works through you. Get in tune with the spirit within you, unify with it, know what you want to accomplish, then let the spiritual power produce it for you. Jesus said, "The Father knows what things you have need of before you ask Him." Emerson said, "The finite alone hath wrought and suffered; the Infinite lies stretched in smiling repose." Your job is *what;* God's job is HOW. Each to his own job. Let the spirit inspire you; then let it flow through you and do the job. Develop these steps and you will have spiritual power.

Consciousness Conditioner for Spiritual Awareness

My power comes from within. My power is of the spirit. I recognize the source of all things within me.

I unify with the presence and power of Spirit. I am a whole person. I can do all things through the inner power which strengthens me. I am attuned to spirit. I am divinely guided. I am an integral part of the One Power. I am a mature and balanced individual.

There is no place where God leaves off and I begin. We are one. I see the whole picture now. I grasp the larger scope of things. I am devoted to the upward path. I worship that which is greater than I. I adore the perfect order, symmetry and system of the universe. I live joyously, with insight and dedication. I express life freely at all times. I release all human limitation. I cooperate with spirit in action through me now. And so it is.

STEP TWO

Mental Power

WE LIVE in a universe of mental activity. There is no limit to the scope of the mind. The One Mind—God—is limitless; the individual expressions of It have the potential of being so. Your mind is the gateway to wisdom, knowledge, understanding and power.

If you want to experience any particular thing, you must first know it in your mind. Under the same law, anything that is known and accepted in your mind—consciously and subconsciously—must become a fact in your experience. The immutable Law of Cause and Effect is always working. The cause is always in the mind. Thoughts, ideas, attitudes, opinions, convictions, feelings, urges, desires and decisions are all mental activities.

Your mind is a wonderful tool with which you mold objects and experiences out of the raw stuff of unformed intelligence. What is your mind? Don't

119

worry about explaining it. It *is,* so use it intelligently and well. Don't be afraid of it. Make it your friend. Recognize it, train it, discipline it, praise it and use it, and it will serve you as a good and faithful servant.

Your mind has two major interrelated functions —the conscious and the subconscious. Sometimes we seem to have two minds, but it is really, more accurately, one mind working in two ways. The conscious mind selects, chooses and initiates action. It thinks, reasons and reaches conclusions. The subconscious mind is the powerhouse within you. It is the creative power of the universe working through you. It is limited and conditioned only by the specific thought patterns of the conscious mind. Memory, intuition and feeling are all seated in the subconscious mind. Personal power comes from learning to coordinate these two marvelous functions of your mind. Step Two and Step Three both help us do this.

Right now we will deal with the five steps to mental power:

1. *CLARITY*. Think definitely, specifically and logically.

2. *HUMOR.* Look at the lighter side of things.

3. *PERSEVERANCE.* Become great by keeping eternally at it.

4. *THOROUGHNESS.* Whatever you do, do it well.

5. *DETACHMENT.* Do your part and the results will take care of themselves.

Clarity

Get clearly in mind what you want. Form a clear
picture of your desired objective. That which your
conscious mind selects will be accepted and
produced by the subconscious. Visualize clearly and
think logically, building your conclusions step by
step. When you build a house you start with a clear
set of blueprints. The same process must be followed
in the use of your mind. The conscious function is
the *instruction department;* the subconscious function is the *construction* department. Effectiveness
depends upon clear instructions. Your subconscious
can only do what you tell it to. Reason logically,
select wisely, and formulate clearly. These are necessary steps in clear thinking.

Humor

"Laugh and the world laughs with you, weep and
you weep alone." This familiar saying just about
tells the whole story. The ponderous approach to life
may produce certain results, but you will never
know what real power is until you develop the light
touch. Power and people automatically flow to the
person who can laugh at himself. Take your work
seriously but yourself, never. "The man worthwhile

is the man who can smile when everything goes dead wrong," proclaimed the poet Edgar Guest. "A merry heart doeth good like a medicine. A broken spirit drieth the bones," says the Proverb. There is no doubt about smiles, laughter and infectious good humor being absolute essentials in your development of personal power.

Perseverance

Discipline your mind to reason through to conclusions. Discipline yourself to carry each task through to completion, no matter how onerous it may be. Otherwise it will plague you until you finish it. Life, energy and intelligence circulate through us freely when we follow through and finish what we start. The difference between success and failure is often a matter of just keeping at it. Keep going until you drop, then get up and take another step. The spirit within you is indomitable; use it. If you get stuck on a tough problem, put it into the subconscious and let it work on it for you, then come back to it later. Sooner or later the answer will be there, but never abandon it. Perseverance is essential for your continued growth.

Thoroughness

"Trifles make perfection, and perfection is no trifle," said Michelangelo. Attention and care must be part of every activity. The world doesn't pay off on slipshod methods and sloppy workmanship. Make yourself responsible for every detail. There is nothing worse than a job half done. This is as bad as being only half right. "Whatsoever your hand finds to do, do it with all your might, as unto the Lord and not unto men." In other words, do a good, thorough job to please the high standards within you. Promotions go to the boys who accept full responsibility for seeing that things are done right. In whatever you do, "leave no stone unturned."

Detachment

Do your job because you want to do it. Give it all you have and don't worry about results. They will automatically be good when you have fulfilled the rest of the requirements. Don't be too concerned about recognition or material rewards. These will come at the right time. Keep yourself free inside, untroubled by details, opinions and outer concerns. Don't let the trivia of life separate you from the magnificence which is all around you just waiting to be expressed. Avoid compromise to gain material advantage. Get quiet and spend time with the real you within. Free yourself from the cacophony and confusion of too much civilization. March to the rhythm of your own drum. "To thine own self be true, and it must follow as the night the day, thou canst not then be false to any man."

Consciousness Conditioner for Mental Attunement

My thought is clear. My mind is attuned to the One Mind—the Source of all intelligence and power. I open my eyes and I see clearly. I think in a straight line. I reason logically. I reach sensible conclusions. All confusion is dissolved from my thoughts. I clarify my viewpoints. I know where I am going. I laugh with life today. I see the humor in every situation. My heart is light as I go diligently and thoroughly about my father's business. I figure things out in my mind. I put my conscious and subconscious faculties to work. I am in tune with the presence and the power. I am a complete being. I assume mental dominion today. And so it is.

STEP THREE

Emotional Power

You NEVER really know a thing until you respond to it emotionally. Feeling is the secret. Thought by itself cannot come to life. There must be a response to it. Thought must be fertilized by feeling. Thought plus feeling produces conviction. Conviction produces results. Clarity of thought plus intensity of feeling are the twin keys to personal power.

As we have seen, the rational processes are the province of the conscious mind, while the emotional responses are generated from the subconscious mind. The person who feels deeply invariably has great personal power, provided that he knows how to control and use his feelings constructively.

Energy and power are released through the emotional nature. Your emotions are the motors which run the machine. Uncontrolled, they vibrate destructively, producing weakness, confusion and sickness. Properly harnessed and used, however, they are the manufacturing plant for health, happiness, success and achievement. Your emotional power can make or break you.

Control is maintained in the conscious mind. Thought provides the plan. Emotions are the power which produces. Thought must handle feeling. Step Two on "Mental Power" and Step Three on "Emotional Power" are for the purpose of teaching you how to understand and use your mind, consciously and subconsciously.

There are many feelings, desires, urges, drives and motives working in our emotional field. Although we may never fully understand them, we can certainly learn to control and use them. These five points are essential to personal emotional power.

1. *LOVE.* The greatest thing in the world.

2. *FAITH.* The power that moves mountains.

3. *PEACE.* That quiet state beyond understanding.

4. *BALANCE.* The maintaining of all things in perfect relationship.

5. *ENTHUSIASM.* The awareness of being God-filled.

Love

Love is affirmative emotional attachment to an idea. Love is the longing of life to express itself.

Love makes the world go around. Love is the one supreme emotional feeling. With love all things are possible. Without love we will never get anywhere. Love is the cement of human relations. Love is the flower of life. Love is the divine ingredient. Love unifies us with all living things. We must take literally the statement, "Love thy neighbor as thyself." This implies, of course, that we must love ourselves —after loving that which makes us what we are: God indwelling. These three, then, are essential to the development of personal power: Love God; love your fellowman; and love yourself—the real Self within.

Faith

Faith is an affirmative attitude of mind which cannot conceive of its opposite. Belief, trust, reliance and conviction are all aspects of faith. Faith is knowing. Faith gives you confidence in yourself. If you don't have faith in yourself, no one else is going to. Trust the power within you. Go all the way with your ideas. Faith is the first ingredient for success. Faith dissolves fear and all negative emotions. Build your faith daily. Authority springs from a strong inner faith. Never say die; never give up. Live in constant assurance that all good things are waiting to happen to you. Whatever needs to be done, you can do. "Faith is the substance of things hoped for, the evidence of things not seen."

Peace

"All things proceed from the quiet mind." Seek "the peace that passeth all understanding." Learn to be still and know that the power within is God. Calm, quiet, peace—silence. Walk beside the still waters and lie down in the green pastures of the Spirit. "Abide in the shadow of the Almighty." Develop that inner serenity and tranquillity which is the source of all power. Never react to the turbulence and confusion of outer activity; act always from the center of inner peace within you. Approach each problem with calm and quiet assurance. Let the winds flow and the waves toss. They have nothing to do with you. Rise above the embattled plain and say, "Peace, be still." "Peace I give unto you, not as the world giveth, give I unto you." The kingdom of peace is within you.

Balance

Maintain a balanced relationship between your thoughts, your feelings, and your actions. Keep an even keel at all times. Do not let the pendulum swing too far. Follow the middle path. Get on the beam and stay there. Keep your thoughts and feelings under control. Examine your motives. Act from a center of inner integrity. Curb your urges, appetites and desires. Be strong and definite in your feelings and attitudes, but always suggest more than you actually express. Don't let yourself be carried away by the wrong things. Stay in the driver's seat. Know who you are, and always be aware of what you are doing. Work toward perfect balance of spirit, mind and body. Establish and express wholeness and balance.

Enthusiasm

Catch on fire with your ideas. Enthusiasm means literally, "possessed by a god." Enthusiasm is contagious. Enthusiasm is spiritual, mental and emotional thrust. Enthusiasm enables you to cut through countless difficulties. Enthusiasm is interest and joy in action. Enthusiasm releases your power potential. Enthusiasm colors your world with a rosy hue. Enthusiasm lifts you above the humdrum and the commonplace. Enthusiasm is your release of the power of expectancy. Enthusiasm provides you with the vital and dynamic energy which accomplishes all good things. Enthusiasm is the favorable wind which blows you into port. Enthusiasm is God in action through you.

Consciousness Conditioner for Emotional Power

I feel good today. I control and release the infinite power potential which is always available within me. *I love life and I love to live it. I am affirmative, happy and joyous at all times. I have a deep inner conviction of peace, power and plenty. I have a capacity to know all things and to do all things. Divine energy vibrates through my entire being. I am invincible.*

I luxuriate in inner peace. I express quiet authority. I can do all things through the great inner Self which strengthens me. I am right inside. I am a bright and scintillating star. I operate on God-power. I know that "God's in His heaven, and all's right with the world." I enthusiastically embrace every challenge that comes my way. I am launched into the unlimited wonderland of purposeful activity. I go into orbit now. And so it is.

Physical Power

YOUR BODY is the tangible expression of what you are. It is the temple of the living spirit. Your body is your soul in visible form. Your body is a mechanical masterpiece, but it is much more than that. Your body is the result of what you are inside. Spirit, mind, emotion and substance are its components. Your body is the instrument through which you express yourself. Your body is a tool to be used for accomplishing mighty works.

You are more than your body, but your body is no less than an expression of your consciousness. It reacts to everything that you know, think and feel. It is the effect of your inner wholeness—or lack of it. Your mind forms, maintains and activates your body. Your body is eager and willing to do your bidding, and it will do so as long as it is able. It is up to you to take care of it so that you will have it as long as you need it. The Greeks taught that the ideal

131

relationship is a sound mind in a sound body. We have seen in the previous three steps how to develop a sound mind. In this step we will learn how to develop and maintain a sound, strong and healthy body. This is absolutely essential in the development of maximum personal power.

Health means wholeness. Your wholeness is the result of perfect integration and coordination of spirit, mind and body. Discordant mental and emotional states destroy the cells of the body and make it susceptible to disease, and harmonious emotional states make it possible for the healing flow of spirit to replenish and maintain the various bodily systems in efficient working order. Consciously cooperate with nature in taking care of your body.

These five steps will give you physical health, strength and power:

1. *DISCIPLINE.* Train and direct your abilities and powers.

2. *CARE.* Recognize, bless and praise your magnificent body.

3. *REST.* Take time to re-charge your batteries.

4. *EXERCISE.* Keep active. Nature says, "Use it or lose it."

5. *DIET.* Eat wisely. Nourish yourself with wholesome food.

Discipline

Your body can be trained to do anything you want it to do. Train your body to obey your will. Condition it into perfect coordination and response. Teach your body the skills of purposeful movement and action. Establish control over your body's appetites and demands. Your body loves discipline. It needs a clear pattern upon which to form itself. It responds more efficiently to definite and specific training. Reflexes can be quickened and sharpened by systematic training. Proper carriage and posture result from conscious attention. Bodily skills can be developed through practice. Your body has no will of its own. It cannot refuse to do your bidding. Discipline it so that it always responds as you wish it to.

Care

Be proud of your body. Keep it clean and pure. Develop a program of strict personal hygiene. Do the things that provide a maximum sensible care for your body. Pay particular attention to grooming. Take pride in your appearance. Be at your best at all times. Keep your body bright, firm and fresh through proper care. Use sensible aids to beauty and attractiveness. Cosmetics, perfumes, lotions, haircuts and manicures can all assist you in developing personal power at the bodily level. Physical attractiveness can be greatly assisted by learning how to dress properly. Wear the best clothes you can afford. A well-dressed person definitely has more personal power. Pay attention to quality and styling. Be good to your body and it will be good to you.

Rest

Take time for rest and re-filling. Recharge your body at frequent intervals. Use the healing power of relaxation. Take time out and let nature take over. It knows what to do to replenish and refresh your body. Cooperate with it. Get all the sleep you need. Practice the "art of sitting loose."* Be still and become aware of the life power within you. Don't wear yourself out with purposeless activity. Sit still and enjoy life once in awhile. Withdraw from intensive activity and lie down occasionally when the going gets rough. Don't push yourself. Learn the art of taking minute vacations. Take catnaps. Walk away from trouble and work if you need to. Heed your body. It will tell you when it needs rest. Take it.

Exercise

Your body needs to be used. Every muscle should have some exercise every day. If your work doesn't

---

*See the author's larger work *Your Thoughts Can Change Your Life*, Wilshire Book Co., 1961.

provide it, it is up to you to provide it with special exercise. You should go through a simple set of conditioning exercises at least once a day—every day. Exercise is most beneficial when done regularly. Deep breathing, stretching, knee-bends, touching your toes, push-ups, rotating the neck and trunk, swimming, walking and running will all help you develop physical power. Exercise can be fun. Make a game of it. Dancing is exercise. Go dancing. Play games with your family—ping-pong, badminton, tennis. Go bowling. Take up handball or golf. Get up a baseball game. Go climb a mountain. Take a walk. Take time to exercise. Give your body a chance. You will have more personal power on every level when you keep your body in trim.

Diet

Let's face it: there are certain things that are good for you to eat, and others that are not. Find out about food. At the physical level, you are pretty much what you eat. You can't build a good house out of bad material. You can't build a good body without good food. There are many excellent books which explain the proper balance of proteins, carbohydrates, fats, minerals, etc. Work out a good basic diet that meets your needs. Avoid heavy, sweet and starchy foods. Steer clear of refined foods in favor of those which are in their more natural state. Fresh fruits and vegetables, preferably organically grown, are an important part of your diet. Take advantage of the abundant selection of magnificent fuel which nature has provided for our consumption. Do a little adventuring on the food front. Your body will appreciate your care in feeding it. It will respond with strength and power.

Consciousness Conditioner for Physical Strength

I give thanks for my strong and useful body. I feel the surge of life and power through every fibre of it. My blood stream carries the currents of life into every cell. There is no limit to my strength. I can lift the world today. I am plugged into the universal circuits of energy and power. My body is responsive and cooperative. I take care of my body. I train it. I purify it. I exercise it thoroughly and wisely. I am a spiritual being made up of all the elements of universal substance. I am responsible for the condition of my body. I do my best to maintain a sound mind and a sound body. I know they are interrelated. One helps the other. My soul is building a stately mansion of my body today. I live in this bodily house with dignity and strength. And so it is.

Material Power

THINGS ARE thoughts in material form. Matter is spirit made visible. Our world is the projection of our consciousness. We must control our world or it will control us. Material things are neither good nor bad. They just are. It all depends upon our attitude toward them and our use of them. This includes money.

Your material power depends upon seeing the material world of manifestation in its proper perspective. In Part II we have seen that each of us exists on five separate and distinct, but interrelated, levels. It is necessary that we generate power on each of the levels if we are to be a whole person. Spirit is the source of power, mind is the use of it, feeling steps it up to meet the need, the physical body is its personal form, and the material world is its expression in multiplicity and variety. There is no limit to the forms that spirit can produce. The important thing to remember is that they are produced by an action of the mind using the Infinite Intelligence.

Therefore, you have material power when you relate yourself intelligently. Remember, prosperity is first a state of consciousness, and only secondarily material expression. God loves a prosperous man. You should have and experience every good thing you need. But remember, exert material power by possessing things; don't let things possess you. All material things—money, clothes, houses, automobiles—all possessions—are in a state of transition—congealed temporarily for you to use and enjoy. Be glad when they appear; have no concern when they disappear.

Your material power comes from your independent attitude toward material things. Work to express yourself, and your material world will reflect what you are. Accumulation is unnecessary. Material substance flows, formulated by your consciousness—your thoughts, ideas, desires and plans. The important thing to remember is that you have an existence completely independent of your physical body and your material world. Jesus said, "These things shall pass away, but my words shall not pass away. . . . In the world ye shall have tribulation, but be of good cheer, I have overcome the world."

Of course, our material possessions cannot just be ignored; they must be taken care of. These five steps tell us how to do that:

1. *STEWARDSHIP*. Take good care of what God has given you.

2. *ORDER*. "Order is heaven's first law." Maintain it.

3. *EASE*. Learn to "let go and let God" work through you.

4. *EFFICIENCY*. Imitate Nature. She does everything in the most efficient way possible.

5. *EFFECTIVENESS*. Work with purpose. Make what you do pay off.

Stewardship

Be faithful over a few things and you will become master of many. Take good care of your possessions. Bless them and praise them, even though they seem to be only inanimate objects. Spiritual intelligence indwells them. A prospective buyer remarked about the fact that the carpeting in a certain house was just like new even though it was nearly twenty years old. "You see, it couldn't wear," the seller, a recent widow replied. "My husband and I expressed only love in this house. There was no friction here." Try this principle. It works. Material things respond to care, love and harmony. Take care of your things. You see, we don't own our possessions at all. They have been loaned to us to use. Possession is a privilege. Privilege entails responsibility. Be a good steward.

Order

Maintain order at all times. Order is evidence of your authority, control and power. Confusion in your surroundings and affairs indicates confusion in your consciousness. Disorder is just bad business. Material things are tools, that's all. Take good care of your tools. Have a place for everything and keep everything in its place. Orderly, harmonious surroundings increase your power on all the other levels of your being. A well-kept house, for instance, brings peace, security and happiness to those who dwell in it. When you maintain order, it is evidence that you know what you are doing. People as well as the flow of material supply are automatically attracted to orderly surroundings. Do you want to develop personal power? Come to order!

Ease

Jesus said, "I of myself do nothing. The father that dwelleth within me; he doeth the work." Stress, strain and struggle have no place in the creative process. They just show that you are getting in your own way. Flow with life—don't try to go upstream.

The power flows *with* the tide. Time and the natural forces of nature and the creative process will do nearly everything for you if you provide good, clear ideas plus trust and patience. Do not confuse busyness with accomplishment. Running around in circles generates a lot of activity, but it accomplishes very little. Don't press when you come to bat. It's the long, smooth swing that produces the home run. It is the smooth, steady stride that covers the distance. Get still inside. An old oriental proverb states, "All things proceed from the quiet mind."

Efficiency

Anything worth doing is worth doing well. Sloppy workmanship just doesn't pay off. There is a right way to do everything. Learn the laws and procedures first, and depart from them only when your experience and skill develop improvements. Carelessness is evidence of inner deterioration. Discipline your mind, control your emotions, and direct your actions. There is no other way to personal power. The efficient way is the fastest way. Don't worry about shortcuts. Do the job and do it right. Take pride in your work. Put your stamp upon your surroundings. Be definite, specific and clean-cut. Make it very clear what you mean. Get rid of excess baggage — intellectually, emotionally, and materially. Get in trim. Stay shipshape at all times.

Effectiveness

The effective person is the one who handles himself and his material possessions well. There should be a reason for everything you do. Work for results. Make your life mean something. Plan to produce results. Get some objectives in mind. Set some goals. Formulate some plans. Build toward something. Establish authority. Be a leader. Make things add up. Show a profit in everything you do. Do good for others. Work to be of service. Produce things that are useful. Help people. Express yourself. Sharpen your curiosity. Move forward. Welcome change. Keep moving. Enjoy life. Learn to live. Learn to laugh. Share with others. Praise God. Give thanks for the privilege of playing this wonderful game of life.

Consciousness Conditioner for Material Expression

I give thanks for the wonder of life. I praise God from whom all blessings flow. Whatever my hand finds to do, I do it mightily and well. I am a good workman. I produce results. I am a good steward. I am trustworthy and responsible. I take good care of those things entrusted to me. I maintain perfect order at all times. I project right action in all that I do. I relax and release. I flow with the main

*stream. I am a co-creator with God. I give thanks
for the abundance which is mine. I have a high
consciousness. I produce the best and I take good
care of it when it arrives. I see God in everything.
I am amazed and grateful. I thrill to the beauty of
life. I live life abundantly now. And so it is.*

Organize

"**K**EEP YOUR eyes open today," my father used to admonish me frequently.

"Why?" I would inevitably ask.

"So you can see," he would laugh, enjoying the old chestnut upon which I always "bit."

But the lesson was, and is, a sound one. You can't see where you're going unless your eyes are open — any more than you can see what you're doing unless you organize your thoughts and ideas. Clearly organized plans are the eyes of your mind. Form them clearly and carefully. You can't accomplish very much unless you know what you're doing.

Designing, planning and organizing is the most important phase of any project. You wouldn't think of building a house without first drawing a set of plans. You can't build anything without a blueprint. You simply must know what you're doing, whether it is making a speech, putting on a sales campaign, or building a bridge. *Things don't just happen. We "happen" them.*

There is no substitute for clearly organized thought. Bring your mind to a focus. Be definite and specific. Fuzzy thinking doesn't pay off. There is no percentage in going off half-cocked. The winner always knows what he is doing. The loser never knows what hit him because he wasn't ready for what was ahead. Many talented and gifted persons are missing the boat because they haven't organized their ideas, their energies and their actions. Nothing good ever came out of confusion. It is pointless to "ride off in all directions at once," when a little intelligent organization can get us on the right track toward success and achievement.

"Snafu — situation normal: all fouled up" — and "tarfu — things are really fouled up" — may have made good jokes in the Army, but they are completely needless and wasteful. Inefficiency and ineffectiveness can be eliminated. You can express power and authority when you organize first, then act. The point is made, isn't it? Let's *do* it!

There are five steps in the organizational process:

1. *SELECTION.* Choose what you want to do.

2. *INVESTIGATION.* Find out all you can about it.

3. *CLASSIFICATION.* Sort out the ideas and information you need.

4. *CRYSTALLIZATION*. Formulate a definite plan of procedure.

5. *REVISION*. Change the plan when necessary but never abandon the design of your original intention.

Selection

You are always confronted with a choice. There is always "more than one way to skin a cat." It is up to you to decide. Choose your goal and move steadily toward it. Draw a bead on the target and shoot straight. Get clearly in mind what you want and keep your mind focused on it. Be definite and specific in your objective. Let nothing deter you as you move steadily along toward success and accomplishment of what you want to be and do.

Investigation

Knowledge is power. The man of authority is the man who knows what he is doing. Master your subject. Find out all you can about it; find out all you can about yourself. Ask some intelligent questions. Do some study and reading. Be sure you are up on things. Avoid making a fool of yourself just because you don't know all that you should. Get smart! Do some observing, some experimenting and some thinking. No one can ever take from you what you know.

Classification

After you have thought, read, studied and observed yourself full, it is time to think yourself clear — to take stock of what you know and find out how it fits into your plan of success. Make a filing cabinet of your mind. Keep the clutter cleared up. Remember what you choose to, and consciously forget a lot of the junk that clogs the brain. Be a friend to your memory and it will be a friend to you. You are more powerful and efficient when your mind is well stocked and well organized.

Crystallization

Now that you have completed your background, it is time to distill all that you know into a simple and definite plan for action. You know WHAT you want, now plan HOW to go about getting it. Develop your plan. Think it through, and rehearse it step by step. Be prepared for every contingency. Leave nothing to chance. Know what you are doing, and develop a strong conviction that you can do it. This is an unbeatable combination.

Revision

Keep your plan constantly in mind, but do not be afraid to change it if necessary. Be prepared for any contingency. The unexpected IS TO BE EX-PECTED in life. Be flexible, ready to move in whatever direction is necessary. Don't be afraid to "ad lib." The payoff comes to the fellow who is able to think on his feet. Learn the rules, but also learn when to break them. Make your plans and mark out your procedures, but don't be afraid to strike out into unexplored territory when you need to. Be bold, and mighty forces will surge through you. Just be sure you know where you are going.

Follow these suggestions and you will be an organized person. Now let's make it permanent by conditioning the consciousness — your whole being — to accept the idea of ORGANIZATION.

Consciousness Conditioner

I am a well-organized person. I know who I am, where I am going, and how to get there. I keep ever before me the image of what I want to be and do. I know exactly what I am doing at all times. I am never caught off base. I think clearly and intelligently and I respond calmly and quietly. Confusion is dissolved and order, harmony and balance are established in my mind.

I choose wisely everything I say and do. I exercise the power of selection. I am alert, awake and aware. I am on the beam. I investigate and study. I am up on all things pertaining to my interests. I know what I am doing. I arrange what I know. I keep my life in order. I move steadily ahead toward my objective. In my mind, I am already there. *I am a well-organized person now. And so it is.*

Visualize

"**D**o you see?" a high school teacher of mine used to ask after explaining some point in the lesson.

"Yes sir, I see," stammered the hapless student who had been called upon.

"What do you see?" shot back the instructor. If we could explain it clearly, we would be praised and commended. But if we were vague and fuzzy in our thinking, the fat was in the fire, and we were drilled until we could really see what our mentor was talking about. He had no patience with wobbly thinking. We either knew what we were talking about or we didn't. This was easy to tell when we tried to explain it so that someone else could "see" what we had in mind.

And so it is in life. The reason we have so many mixed-up situations in our lives is because we are not seeing clearly—not understanding, and not forming clear images of what we want to experience.

"Do you get the picture?" a very successful businessman of my acquaintance always asks when he finishes explaining a plan or project. He believes that you can't possibly accomplish anything unless you can actually see it as an accomplished fact before you start. He pictures everything down to the minutest detail, and his plans always work out for him.

I myself have learned to form a picture of whatever I want to do as a vital step toward bringing it about. Whenever I have failed to complete the inner picture, I have had trouble bringing the outer one into manifestation. Remember: WE EXPERIENCE EXACTLY WHAT IS IN OUR MINDS. It is essential to form not only a mental, but a VISUAL equivalent of your objective or desire. See it — flash it in complete form upon the sensitive photographic plate of your inner mind and it will develop into a full-scale, three-dimensional actuality in your world of experience. Use your imaging faculty to do this. That is what it is for.

I use this technique constantly in planning lectures and writing books. I always see a book in its complete form before I start writing it. I see great numbers of people reading it, enjoying it, and profiting from its content. I never give a talk without seeing the entire outline, delivery, acceptance and effect upon the audience clearly in my mind. Visualization played a vital part in the building of my home. One day it stood there — an exact replica of the picture I had long held in my mind. On one occasion I demonstrated a large sum of money simply by counting thousand-dollar bills in my mind until I could see great numbers of them in my possession.

Visualization works. Use it. "See the picture!" Here are five steps to help you:

1. *FORMULATION.* Give body and form to your idea.

2. *PICTURIZATION.* See the entire picture completed.

3. *CLARIFICATION.* Work out the kinks and perfect your plan in your mind.

4. *IDENTIFICATION.* Become one with your objective.

5. *IMAGINATION.* Make your experience as real in your mind as you want it to be in your actual manifestation.

Formulation

Build the body of your objective. Make it tangible and real. See it, hear it, touch it, taste it, smell it, lift it. Know that it is there. Give it form and dimension. Recognize it. Respect it. Possess it. Use it. Make a place for it in your mind and it will find its own place in your world. Your ideas, thoughts and plans are the framework — the bones and skeleton.

Now put some flesh on it. Make a living, breathing body out of your idea. Go all the way with the creative process.

Picturization

Your conscious mind is the camera. Your subconscious mind is the film. Focus your thought. See what you want to see. Concentrate your attention. Get the proper lighting, composition and balance. SEE the picture and photograph it. Or draw it and paint it. Give it color and tone—warmth and life. Your thoughts and feelings are the pencils and brushes which you, the artist, use in creating your picture. Make your picture a beautiful one. It is easier to do a good job than a bad one. You live with every picture you paint. You ARE the picture.

Clarification

Go over every detail of your plan or project. Do a thorough, careful job. Leave nothing to chance. Take your time and do it right. Care taken in the planning and visualizing stages will pay dividends later on. Rome wasn't built in a day and neither were you—and neither are your plans and projects. Sculpture the finished product out of the substance of your thought and feeling. Cut out the twists and turns, and establish straight, clean lines. Face facts;

clarify issues involved. Be definite, specific and objective. Cut out everything that doesn't help you achieve your goal.

Identification

Actually become one with your objective. Absorb it and let it absorb you. You ARE the living expression of your idea. Eat, sleep and live that which is most important to you. "Act as though you were and you will be." Identify yourself with happiness. Identify yourself with success. LOOK like what you want to be. Act like it. Talk like it. Eliminate everything from your life that is not contributing to building you into the image and likeness of what you want to be. Get on the constructive side of life. Believe in the good things of life and they will appear in your life. Identify yourself with the object of your desire.

Imagination

Use your imagination. It is one of your most valuable tools. It is your creative power, and is working 24 hours a day building images of the thoughts and ideas which you feed it with your conscious mind. Learn to "daydream" consciously and constructively. Build "castles in the air." Develop the use of your imagination. It must be controlled, but it is the gateway to all wonderful things. It knows no limitation whatsoever. Put your imagination to work on your problems, your goal, your objective, your dream, your ideal. Picture them as already completed facts in your experience. Turn them over to your imagination and let the great creative power within produce them in your life.

Consciousness Conditioner

I see everything in my life from the highest point of view. I have a clear picture of exactly the way things should be. I learn to see only what I want to experience. I see only good now. I dissolve everything that doesn't live up to the specifications of constructive right action. I am at work building more stately mansions in my soul. My mind and my imagination are engaged in great projects. I am identified with ideas and projects of true and noble purpose. Everything is clear to me now. I see clearly where I am going and what I have to do. My eye is single and my world of experience is full of light. I turn all of my ideas over to the creative power of my imagination. I am constructively and creatively involved in the business of living. I am a whole person now. And so it is.

STEP EIGHT

Energize

THE LIFE force is a cosmic, electric current running through everything. Life is energy. It must be used; it must be lived. Energy is expressed through intelligence, light and vibration. Our power comes from the energy potential within us. We all have the same universal potential upon which to draw. It is our personal use of it that varies. Our purpose here is to learn how to make better use of our potential—how to let more of the stuff of life flow into all that we are and do—how to ENERGIZE.

We draw energy into our minds, bodies and experiences through the nature of our thought and feeling. Let's learn to think and feel in a constructive manner. This will plug you into the creative circuits of life and give you the energy to do whatever you want to do. Constructive thought and feeling keep your batteries charged. It is through your mind that the dynamic, vitalizing vibrations of cosmic power flow into you. Let's get on working terms with the plus factor.

Interest, desire and expectancy are essential life-giving attitudes. Observe the energy and vitality in children. Why? Because they are interested in everything around them. Every moment provides a new experience. They are "with it." They are plugged in to the inner electricity. Animals, too, are constantly aware of everything around them. Let's wake up, take a lesson from the kids and the pets and get interested in everything all over again. You'll be surprised how much you learn and how much fun it is.

How much do you care whether you succeed or not? How important are things to you? How much do you want to do a good job? All of these questions have to do witih desire, the second of the great energy producers. If you want to do something intensely enough, there isn't anything that can stop you. The universal reservoir of all power, energy and life is yours to draw upon. Your desire is the faucet which turns on the flow. Use it. Let it work for you. That is what it is for. Legitimate desire, coupled with determination and faith, will give you the strength and follow-through to accomplish wonders.

Are you "on fire" with life? Do you give all that you have to what you have to do? If you do, you have enthusiasm. If you don't, it is time you did something about it. Enthusiasm means "filled with God" — or energy — life — strength — good. This is the key: Fill yourself with God — Good — and go ahead and do what you have to do. The energy of life will be right there for you to use.

Here are five steps which will turn it on:

1. *RECOGNITION.* Become aware of a tremendous force working through you.

2. *EXPECTATION.* Know that only good can come to you.

3. *VITALIZATION.* Breathe life and joy into everything.

4. *EMOTIONALIZATION.* Develop a strong conviction and faith.

5. *DEDICATION.* Give yourself to something bigger than you are.

Recognition

Realize that you are not alone. We are all part of a tremendous system of life. We are expressions of it. It works through us in accordance with the level of our thought.

There is no place where it leaves off and we begin. It is what we are. We are that which it is. Know this truth about yourself. Energy and strength flow into you when you recognize that the source of all energy and strength is within you. We are operating at less than 10% of our capacity because we fail to recognize that we have this capacity. Let's remedy that right now.

Expectation

We attract into our lives that which we steadily expect. How many times have you exclaimed, "I knew that would happen!" when disaster falls—thus indicating that you yourself ordered the misfortune. Your thoughts may say one thing, but if your feelings are negative, uncertain or afraid, they determine what is going to happen. We may SAY we expect good, but unless our feelings are in accord, we set up a negative expectation without actually being aware of it. The secret is to consciously establish constructive expectation by bringing our thoughts and feelings into agreement. Eagerly anticipate good as intensely as you once feared evil. Use the power of expectancy to release creative energy into your life.

Vitalization

Paul said, "The letter killeth, but the Spirit giveth life." Put spirit into everything you do. Don't let procedures, details and opinions choke the life out of your project. Keep your objective clearly in mind and drive steadily toward it. Infuse your every action with vitality and strength. Come to life and what you do will be a graphic manifestation of your inner dynamic forces. Life is for living. Live it through your work, your plans, your projects, your goals. Be interested in what you are doing, and don't be afraid to let your excitement show. Others will become infected with your enthusiasm and life will flow freely through everything you do.

Emotionalization

Love life and love the living of it. Love what you are doing. Feel deeply and intensely. Emotion hasn't gone out of style. Warm up inside. Respond with your entire feeling nature. Let your heart expand— embrace the whole world and everyone and everything in it. Let your exultation show. Stir up your creative power and then control its action by consciously directing it for constructive purposes. Sustain your feeling through conviction and faith. Follow through until you achieve success in everything you undertake. Remember, we experience what we feel. Develop the feeling that your desired good is an already accomplished fact in your experience, then let it happen. Achieve your full potential by learning to control and direct your feelings.

Dedication

What is the most important thing in the world to you? Why are you doing what you are doing? What is your purpose in life? Are you working for a larger idea? What is really important to you? Are you a dedicated person? Dedicated to what? This is for each of us to decide. Our dedication is the spiritualization of our ideas—of our lives—and Spirit is the universal energy, the Source of all things. Desire that which is for the best interest of everyone concerned. Work for that which is for the greatest good of the greatest number. "Whatsoever ye do, do it heartily, as to the Lord, and not unto men." (Col. 3:23)

Consciousness Conditioner

I am filled with energy and vitality today. I am alertly and dynamically attuned to life. The free, full flow of spiritual energy is surging through me now. I recognize the Source from which all good flows. I am connected with the circuits of life-giving energy. I vibrate with expectancy. I am completely alive. I am a vital person. I sparkle and scintillate. I joyously sing and exultantly proclaim the wonder and beauty of life. I feel the currents of creativity circulating through my entire being. I channel my life force into completely constructive activities. I dedicate myself to large purpose. My life is teeming with meaning. I live the full and abundant life now. And so it is.

STEP NINE

Realize

THOUGHTS ARE things in their invisible state. Things are thoughts — ideas — feelings — convictions in tangible form. The line between the tangible and the intangible is very fine. We are constantly crossing it with our senses and our minds. When you believe something is real or true it actually becomes so for you.

In this book we are talking about mental and emotional attitudes as the cause of all things, and we are learning the techniques by which we can develop the attitudes which will produce for us whatever we wish to experience in our lives. The net result of the systematic culturing of our attitudes is a strong inner conviction that what we desire is ready and waiting now to actually appear as fact.

When we reach this realization, we will spend our time strengthening our inner attitudes — working at the point of cause, rather than vainly striving to make things happen. The creative law of life

162

is constantly working to give life, growth and manifestation to the seeds which we plant through our belief and conviction. Realization of this truth is the essence of wisdom; it is the secret of success. It is your guarantee of peace and happiness. Realization of inner creative action ensures constructive achievement.

When you have an idea or are working toward something, it is already real. The fact that it is in your mind makes it so. That is the secret. REALIZE that this is true. Accept your good. Release it. Give thanks that it is already true. Maintain peace of mind about it and let it emerge into form. Let the seeds of your spiritual, mental and emotional conviction take root. BECOME the thing which you want to experience. This is true realization—when there is no longer any doubt, concern or speculation concerning the outcome of your plan. You just KNOW everything is working out in right action and perfect order. There is tremendous creative power in faith. Use it. Realization makes it available to you.

Use these five steps to develop your Realization:

1. *APPRECIATION*. Give thanks for the abundance which is yours.

2. *COMPLETION*. Build an inner conviction of acceptance.

3. *VERIFICATION*. Know that what you desire is already true.

4. *EXPANSION*. Extend your consciousness to include new experience.

5. *CONSUMMATION*. Have faith that your desired good is an accomplished fact.

Appreciation

Learn to give thanks for good received BEFORE you receive it. Be grateful for everything. Make thanksgiving a way of life. Praise the power within you which is producing all good things in your life. Praise the good efforts of those who help you. Give thanks that you are you, and thank other people for being what they are. Get into the habit of blessing things. Look for ways to show your appreciation. Say prayers of thanks. Never miss an opportunity to express gratitude. Say appreciative things. Write thank-you letters. Send congratulatory telegrams. Increase your good by expanding your circle of appreciation. Know that God IS blessing everything. Thank you. You are welcome.

Completion

See the whole picture. Get the feeling that the project is completed before you actually start outer work on it. Complete the journey in your mind before you take the first step. Round it out. Think right about it. Feel right about it. Speak right about it. Strengthen the weak places. Firm up the soft spots. Tie up the loose ends. Don't just pretend — actually develop a strong conviction of accomplishment and completion. Think and speak in the present tense. Don't postpone the completion of your project or the achievement of your objective. Win the race in your mind and you cannot possibly ever lose it. Do a complete job on yourself. "Act as though you are, and you MUST be."

Verification

Remove all doubt.

> *Accentuate the positive,*
> *Eliminate the negative,*
> *Latch onto the affirmative,*
> *And don't mess with mister in-between.* *

When fears, doubts and uncertainties try to creep in, close the door on them. Constantly strengthen your affirmative attitudes. Keep accepting. Keep knowing. Bring your entire consciousness into line. Believe in yourself.

> *If you can trust yourself when all men doubt*
> *you*
> *Yet make allowance for their doubting too.* †

---

*Johnny Mercer, "Accentuate the Positive."
†Rudyard Kipling, "If."

Base everything you do upon the assumption that your desired good is already a fact. Correct all situations and circumstances to agree with this premise. "True-up" your life. Get right inside, and the outside will take care of itself.

Expansion

As you grow inwardly, the circle of your experience automatically expands to include whatever you have established in your mind. There is no limit to the good you can experience. Cleanse your consciousness of all doubt and limitation. Make room for new ideas. "Think big and you will be big." You will never have an idea that you are incapable of expressing. Trust yourself and trust the power within you. Listen to your hunches and heed your intuition. Explore your every idea thoroughly, no matter how fantastic it may seem. Become acquainted with it, let it simmer, then get yourself out of the way and give it a chance to happen. Remember, "Man's reach exceeds his grasp." You are better than you think you are. Start believing it.

Consummation

Go all the way with your realization. Unify thought and feeling in complete acceptance. Eat, drink, sleep and live your idea. Marry it. Love it. Absorb it. Give it everything you have. Remove all reservations concerning it. Strengthen your faith through prayer and affirmations. Remember, "Nothing is too good to be true; nothing is too wonderful to happen."* Accept your good completely and let it express through you. Every constructive idea makes you a bigger and better person. Remember, we are the sum total of our thoughts, feelings, hopes, dreams and aspirations. Let's make them good.

Consciousness Conditioner

I realize the glory and beauty of life today. I am one with all good things. I get myself out of the way and let abundance of perfect experience take place through me. I give thanks for the abundance which is mine. I appreciate the great gifts of life. I enjoy them as they are expressed in my experience. I know that what I believe is true—IS true for me. I remove all blocks and limitations, and I let the free, full flow of life fill me with joy and abundance. I am one with that which is greater than I. I exuberantly proclaim the good news. I sing from the mountain tops. I am a whole, happy and complete individual now. And so it is.

---

*See the author's larger work *Your Thoughts Can Change Your Life*, Wilshire Book Co., 1961.

Actualize

THE ROCK-AND-DIRT farmer had taken over the little run-down hillside farm and had developed it to a high point of order, productivity and beauty. He was proudly showing his handiwork to his minister who had come to call.

"You and the Lord have done a fine job here," said the parson approvingly.

"Well, now, thanks, Reverened, that's generous of you to say," returned the farmer, "but you should have seen the place when He was running it alone."

Action is our final step—essential and vital, but no more nor less so than the preceding nine. Paul wisely said, "Faith, if it hath not works, is dead— be ye doers of the word, and not hearers only, deceiving your own selves." Once the foundation is laid, we must proceed to build the house. Ideas are a dime a dozen; so are unfinished projects. Getting hold of a good idea, nurturing it, building it, and strengthening it, are all important, as we have shown, but they are all to no avail unless we do something about it. We must follow through. Action must follow preparation. The boys who pick up the marbles are the ones who play the game. Don't let your dream become shipwrecked on the shallows of discouragement, lethargy or indecision.

> *For of all said words of tongue or pen*
> *The saddest are these: "It might have been."**

If you are to experience the full rewards of life, you must follow through. *You must do something.* You and you alone are the master of your fate—the captain of your soul. No one can think for you, dream for you, plan for you, grow for you, or act for you. There is no such thing as fate, chance or luck. We make our own luck by what we believe and do.

In this final step—Actualize—we are learning how to do what we have been preparing for. The demonstration of our good comes about through a natural process of unfoldment. Let's recognize this, and enjoy each step as it unfolds.

Let's go to work, follow through, and make our dreams come true. Here are the five steps of the process:

1. *ACTIVATION.* Carry out what you have previously planned and accepted.

2. *COMMUNICATION.* Connect your outer action with inner guidance.

---

*John Greenleaf Whittier, "Maude Miller."

3. *PARTICIPATION.* Don't be afraid to get your feet wet or your hands dirty.

4. *CONTINUATION.* Follow through. Go into partnership with God.

5. *DEMONSTRATION.* "It is the Father's good pleasure to give you the kingdom."

Activation

Set your machinery in motion. Once you know what you are doing, go ahead and do it. It is said, "God provides food for every bird but He doesn't drop it in the nest." Go to work. Give it all you've got. It is impossible to become tired through good work. Work is the release of energy for constructive purpose. Activity engenders more activity. Make your plans, get organized, and get going. Use your head, your hand, your foot, your back, and whatever else is necessary to get your creative machinery going and keep it going. There is great pleasure and accomplishment in doing things. Get in the swim. You will be amazed what you can get done when you apply yourself diligently and steadily.

Communication

Keep in constant touch with the intelligence within you. Your job is to translate inner guidance into purposeful action and achievement. Keep the lines of communication open. Express yourself freely and confidently. Speak confidently and authoritatively, backed up by the forces within you. The word has power. Learn to express yourself eloquently. Explain and describe what is within you. Communicate with God, communicate with yourself, communicate with other people. Keep your silence during the formative stages of an idea, but when it bursts forth, let people hear about it. Speak intelligently, directly, and with purpose.

Participation

Get on the team. Play the game. Join the club. Come to the party. Life is a game that must be played. It is no fun being a wallflower or a bench warmer. What are you waiting for? How do you know what you can do until you try? If you want to do something, do it. If someone needs your help, give it. Participation, cooperation and teamwork are essential to success. We are all part of something and we MUST do our part. When we do, everyone is working for everyone else as well as himself and tremendous power is generated. Don't hold back. Pull out the stopper and let's get going.

Continuation

What good does it do to throw the ball only part way? Learn the discipline of following through.

Complete whatever you start, even if you have to make yourself do it. Don't let your life become a junk yard of abandoned dreams. Keep even with the board. Keep firing and you are bound to score.

Again, Kipling has something to say:

> *If you can make one heap of all your win-*
> *nings*
> *And risk it on one turn of pitch-and-toss,*
> *And lose, and start again at your beginnings*
> *And never breathe a word about your loss:*
> *If you can force your heart and nerve and*
> *sinew*
> *To serve your turn long after they are gone,*
> *And so hold on when there is nothing in you*
> *Except the Will which says to them:*
> *"Hold On!"*
> *If you can fill the unforgiving minute*
> *With sixty seconds' worth of distance run,*
> *Yours is the Earth and everything that's*
> *in it,*
> *And—which is more—you'll be a Man,*
> *my son!**

Demonstration

Recognize your good when it arrives. We are always demonstrating what we need, even though it is not

---

*Rudyard Kipling, "If."

what we want. There is often more to be learned from failure than success. Our problems are priceless opportunities to learn and grow. There is no wrong action in life. Everything that happens is right action. We are always experiencing that which gives us the greatest growth. Look for the good in every situation. It is there. We are constantly experiencing the outer evidence of our inner consciousness. Demonstration is constant. If ever we don't like what we are demonstrating, we now have the means to change it. Remember, "The Father knows what things we have need of before we ask."

Consciousness Conditioner

All good things are constantly appearing in my world. I am a living demonstration of that which fills my heart and mind. I am visible evidence and action of that which is greater than I. I work diligently and well to produce good things in my world. I maintain my connection with inner guidance. I constantly seek to express my inner greatness. I joyously participate in the magnificent activity of life. I follow through. I know I live forever, so I do a good job now. I am a living demonstration of all that is good. It is a wonderful thing to be a human being. Everything I do demonstrates this conviction. I am a whole person now. And so it is.

Master Consciousness Conditioner
for Personal Power

I AM a powerful person. I give thanks for my personal power. I am an integrated indidivudal. I am whole. I am unified with the One Source. My power comes from the Infinite Intelligence which indwells me. I have a direct line to headquarters. I am aligned with the One Power.

Spirit flows uninterruptedly through every part of my being. I am a spiritual person, therefore I am a powerful person. I know no limitation or restriction. The surge of power moves me along to true and meaningful accomplishment. I am spiritually aware. I have complete spiritual power.

My mind is attuned to the One Mind. I am a clear thinker. I have unlimited intellectual capacity. I perceive truth. I know. I reason logically. I focus my attention upon meaningful ideas. My thoughts are of the highest order. My mind is as clear as a bell. I have keen mental power.

I feel deeply. I express love at all times. Warmth and good will emanate from me. I have a deep and abiding faith. I believe. I trust. I have confidence in the great order of things. I am eager and willing to do God's bidding at all times. I am quiet and tranquil, experiencing and expressing the "peace that passeth all understanding." I have deep emotional power.

My body is the temple of the living spirit. I am physically strong, mentally awake and morally straight. I am formed according to a perfect pattern. I express perfect organic and functional order. I am filled with dynamic energy. I move gracefully. I act purposefully. I am in tune. I am fit. I am filled with life. I have full physical power.

I look out upon my world and I find it good — very good indeed. I am master of all I survey. The blessings of the Infinite are showered upon me. I receive great gifts. I use them wisely and well. I increase my good. I am a co-creator with God. I am rich in all things. I am humble in all ways. I have abundant material power.

I am a complete person now. I have invincible personal power. And so it is.

How to Use Part II

1. Make Part II your constant companion and read it daily for one month.

2. Keep a supply of this book to give away. Get as many copies as possible into circulation as soon as you can. Each book in circulation increases the benefits the Law of Return will bring to you.

3. Re-read Part II whenever trouble arises, whenever you are faced with a problem, whenever you go to work on a new idea, and whenever you want a lift to get your life back on the right track.

4. Make these Ten Steps your way of life. Talk about them freely. Tell everyone you meet how these Ten Steps are firm steps out of the swamp of confusion onto the path of continual growth. Follow these suggestions and your life will be living proof of their power and effectiveness.

5. Use the Consciousness Conditioners at the end of each chapter regularly and show others how to use them.

6. Every day read some inspirational material written by a truth teacher, such as my own *Daily Power for Joyful Living.*

7. Every day practice a specific aspect of one of the Ten Steps to personal power. Don't let a day go by without concentrating on some point. Each point is a building block in your new life.

8. Practice the Presence, building God Consciousness in your life.

9. Challenge each day to provide you with situations to exercise your growing powers.

10. Use regularly the "Master Consciousness Conditioner for Personal Power."